strictly inclusive

James Murray

A Strictly Inclusive Church

Ark House Press
PO Box 1321, Mona Vale NSW 1660
Australia
Telephone: +61 2 9007 5376
PO Box 47212, Ponsonby, Auckland
New Zealand
Telephone: +64 9 416 8400
arkhousepress.com

Ark House Press, a division of Initiate Media.

© James Murray

ISBN: 9780994551665 (pbk.)

Cataloguing in Publication Data:
Title: Strictly Inclusive
ISBN: 9780994551665 (pbk.)
Subjects: Christian Living, Church Growth
Authors: Murray, James

Printed and bound in Australia
Cover design concept by Nathan Johnson (blackliststudio.com) and layout by initiateagency.com

"Very few things in this world are open to all men. A man's mental caliber decides the studies he can undertake. A man's social class decides the circles amongst which he will move. A man's material wealth determines the possessions he can amass. A man's particular gifts decide the things he can do. But the message of the gospel is open without exception to all men"

- William Barclay

ACKNOWLEDGEMENTS

I'd like to say a special thanks to:

My amazing wife and kids.

My family. Our relentlessly inclusive church and team.

Nathan at Blacklist Studios for the amazing cover art.

For those who love and believe in this message.

James Murray

CONTENTS

The Pelican Feather

We were taking our annual Murray family vacation. At this time we were living in sunny Southern California (suffering for the Lord). The location we loved to go was a magical place called Palm Desert. Picture Las Vegas but less poker machines and dancing girls, and more swimming pools, golf courses and more old people, that my friend is Palm Desert!

I told our six year old Bailey, that the place we were staying had the world's greatest slide (exaggeration may have played a part). It towered towards the heavens and came crashing down in to a crystal clear and extremely warm pool. (I am almost one hundred percent sure that the warmth of the pool was due to the outside temperature and not because of children that swam in it...I hope!) My boy lit up quicker than a chain smoker's cigarette, he was pumped and couldn't wait to arrive at the hotel.

After a few hours of driving through winding desert roads, we finally arrived at our hotel. We had barely put the bags down and my man cub Bailey and I were off to the pool to ride this formidable slide. We reached the pool area and the slide was all that and more. We were about to ascend the staircase and out of nowhere this lifeguard popped up like a David Hasselhoff ninja. "Excuse me sir before you and your son can ride the slide we will need to make sure that he is the required height." We walked over to a cut out billboard of a Pelican wearing sunglasses and his right feather was sticking up in the air. A speech bubble protruding from his head declaring, "You must be this height to ride the slide." Unfortunately my boy stepped up to Pelican feather only to find that he was short of the required height by at least 10 inches. The lifeguard informed us that unfortunately due to the required height he was unable to ride the ride. I can still remember my poor little boy's angelic face looking back up and saying, "It's all right Daddy, I can just swim in the pool." My first thought was, seriously....were you born in a manger? You are such a perfect boy.

You see this story very much relates to how most people feel when it comes to church and the potential idea of a relationship with God. Maybe you've heard about this gracious, loving and kind God, but you've come to church and just as you're about to embark upon this amazing ride called a relationship with God, you suddenly find yourself under this overwhelming idea that in order to go any further you must live up to a certain standard. You have walked away thinking, "Well I guess I'm not cut out for this whole relationship with God thing." The reason I am writing this book is to declare, scream, shout to you a big NOOOOOOOOO. You can begin this relationship with God, you can come to him just the way you are, even with your doubts, fears, brokenness, mistakes, shame and guilt. The truth is there was a cut out billboard Pelican with his feather sticking up demanding that you and I live up to a certain way of living. The truth is we couldn't go any further with God without rising to the standard. However God, because of his love for us, sent his son Jesus. He did not come to erase the Pelican Feather - no he came and rose way above it. In his love and grace he put us up onto his shoulders and proudly sat us there and declared that you can now start this amazing adventure called a relationship with God. Why did he do this? Simple, not because you and I deserved it, He did it because he loved you and loved me!

"But because of his great love for us, God, who is rich in mercy, made us alive with Christ even when we were dead in transgressions—it is by grace you have been saved." (Ephesians 2:4-5)

I heard a pastor once say:

"The Bible is one long story of God meeting our rebellion with his rescue, our sin with His salvation, our guilt with His grace, our badness with His goodness. The overwhelming focus of the Bible is not the work of the redeemed but the work of the Redeemer. Which means that the Bible is not first a recipe for Christian living but a revelation book of Jesus who is the answer to our un-Christian living."

The amazing reality of the gospel is that overwhelming fact that God meets us where we are at' The truth is we need him, but Grace tells us he wants us.

Through this book my endeavor is to clearly display what so many people, and even churches have distorted. God is madly in love with humanity. The message of the gospel is one of freedom from the burdened life. Joy to the anxious mind, redemption for the guilty conscience and inclusion to the rejected soul. Is this too good to be true? No it is just the good news of the gospel.

Because of this fact every church and believer in Jesus should have a big huge bold block letter sign declaring that we are **'Strictly Inclusive',** because we have been strictly included by the love of God.

Through the next few chapters I would love to shed light on what it means to be a strictly inclusive church and a strictly inclusive person. Not just in my own words but reflecting the words God inspired and penned in the Bible and the amazing demonstration of Jesus himself. It was reading the Bible that God radically awakened me to the reality that his church is not strictly exclusive but strictly inclusive. By the end of this I hope you are inspired to pray, think and plan on how we can truly tear down the intimidating walls that man, religion, miss-perception and fear has put up to keep the world out of the church. To reveal the glorious, scandalous, relentless love of Jesus! To preach the strictly inclusive gospel requires a strictly inclusive church.

So here we go!

CHAPTER ONE

Country Club or Hospital?

I don't know if you've ever been to a country club, but it is beautiful! I once was invited by a friend in America to play a game of golf (the Lord's sport) at his Dad's country club. When I arrived I pulled up to a big steel gate with two security guards posted at each side. I am pretty sure they both had crew cuts and silver reflector sunglasses on. One of them approached my car as I sheepishly wound down the window. "Name?"

"Ahhh James Murray."

"Ok sir, your name looks to be on the list, you may now proceed with caution." As I drove in, my jaw dropped. I had never seen more beautiful scenery. Perfectly manicured gardens, opulent houses, there where more expensive cars than all 17 *Fast & the Furious* movies combined! Not to mention the golf course that weaved its way up to the clubhouse. When I arrived at the clubhouse I was met by the bag carriers who did not take too kindly to my outfit. Because at this point I was still wearing my thongs (flip flops for my American friends, don't get too ahead of yourselves) I was yet to put on my golf shoes. Everything about the place was amazing, but I gathered pretty quickly due to the $200,000 dollar country club membership fee that this place wasn't meant for everyone. If anything it was only available to the select few. It was strictly **ex**clusive.

Sad to say but this is most people's perception of the church. That the church is a country club for the morally elite - a gated community for the good. To get in is hard and if you do, you better dress right and behave right, because this isn't a place for just your average anybody. Unfortunately the church can easily be viewed as a moralistic mecca.

The point of the letter Paul wrote to the Galatian church (which I encourage you to read) was to counteract the message that the religious folk had been propagating. The religious where happy to know God and be loved by God, but didn't want to make it a free for all. They felt Paul's approach to God and his love was way too easy, too attainable, too inclusive. They wanted to make sure people had to jump through behavioral, moral, religious hoops before they could get to God. **BUT THAT'S NOT THE MESSAGE OF THE STRICTLY INCLUSIVE GOSPEL OR THE MESSAGE OF A STRICTLY INCLUSIVE CHURCH.**

Paul, inspired by God, writes to aggressively and adamantly oppose that message and he spends this entire letter declaring the simplicity of the gospel and the attainability of God's love is freely given through Jesus.

You see the church is not a country club; it's more like a hospital. Although hospitals are clean in nature they where designed to house and heal sick, broken, hurting people. Jesus declared in the gospels of Matthew, Mark and Luke, "It's not the healthy who need a doctor but the sick." The reason why the church can never be a country club is because the truth is we are all sick. We all need help. With that in mind let's also remember that when you go to a hospital you will typically find two types of people:

1. People who are sick

2. And people who are on the road to recovery

When we really think about it, the church is exactly the same. It is a hospital of hope for humanity. When we go to church let's remember who and what it is designed for. It's designed for the sick. No one walks into a hospital and complains that there are too many sick people around! We should expect that. We need not neglect the fact that we are not visitors who are healthy, happy and whole, but we are also patients in need of the same grace filled attention.

What unites us, as the church is not necessarily our pursuit of goodness, but the realization that none of us are good. But Jesus still loves and accepts us and we trust him by his grace to make us better. He is the doctor and our job is not to make more patients for him through our religious malpractice in the world, but to bring him more patients through our love and service to the world. A Strictly inclusive church is a hospital for humanity. **What does a strictly inclusive church look like to you?**

CHAPTER TWO

Who Am I?

"Paul, an apostle—sent not from men nor by a man, but by Jesus Christ and God the Father, who raised him from the dead— and all the brothers and sisters with me, To the churches in Galatia: Grace and peace to you from God our Father and the Lord Jesus Christ, who gave himself for our sins to rescue us from the present evil age, according to the will of our God and Father, to whom be glory for ever and ever. Amen." (Galatians 1:1-5)

One of my favorite movies of all time is *Zoolander*. Come on, it's brilliant, "I know what will cheer you right up, 'Orange Mocha Frappuccino.'" Haha classic *Zoolander*. In one of the scenes in the movie Derek Zoolander has an identity crisis and looks into a murky puddle one starry night and whispers the words through his blue steel pout, *"Who am I?"*

We laugh at this point in the movie but everyone at one time or another has asked the same question? "Who am I?"

You see in order to determine the activity of a strictly inclusive church we have to establish the identity of the strictly included believer. (I know, deep right!) Truth is so many times in my life my activity has determined who I am.

In the early years of my life in full time church ministry, I really felt God asking me to hand over the youth ministry of which I was the leader. I fought it, convinced it was just some crazy idea in my head. After months of fighting with God I finally gave in and handed over the youth ministry. Most people looking on outwardly would think 'wow such a humble person, so Christ like, he permeates selflessness, Mother Teresa would be jealous of your humility (Okay I'll stop now, but you get the point) but inwardly I was ticked! I thought it was the dumbest mistake of my life. A week or so after the decision I was away snowboarding with my wife and family. At one point during the day I was separated from the pack and found myself alone on a chair lift heading back up the mountain. I don't know if you've ever been on a chair lift alone on a mountain but it is eerily quiet, and as I sat there I prayed, "God what have you done to me?" and it was as if the words had just left my heart I heard a response come straight back into my heart. "James you've taken Isaac to the altar and he is never coming back" and "Don't restrict my Grace to a position." Now if you're not familiar with Old Testament Bible you'll know about an old dude called Abraham who has a son Isaac. Long story short but God asks Abraham to give up his son Isaac and just as he is about to do so, God stops him and gives him back. Truth is in my heart I thought being the humble servant who gave up something so precious God would be moved by my humility and give back what I so humbly gave up. AAAAAHHHH no! You see my identity was wrapped up in my activity, what I did, determined who I was. God was taking me on a journey by showing me first that it's not what I do that determines who I am. It is who I am in Christ that determines what I will do.

I love Eighteenth century Danish Philosopher Theologian Soren Kierkegaard's comment on our struggle with the human ego:

> "THE NORMAL HUMAN EGO IS BUILT ON SOMETHING
> BESIDES GOD. IT SEARCHES FOR SOMETHING
> THAT WILL GIVE IT A SENSE OF WORTH, A SENSE
> OF SPECIALNESS, A SENSE OF PURPOSE AND BUILDS
> ITSELF ON THAT. AND OF COURSE, AS WE ARE
> OFTEN REMINDED, IF YOU TRY TO PUT ANYTHING IN
> THE MIDDLE OF THE PLACE THAT WAS ORIGINALLY
> RESERVED FOR GOD, IT IS GOING TO BE TOO SMALL."

The issue is if your identity is wrapped up in your performance it's almost impossible to become a strictly inclusive person. Why? Glad you asked!

Activity is only viewed successful if it is measured. You measure how good you are at a sport by how many points you gain against the other team. You measure activity in your career by the measurement of what you get paid. You measure your activity on social media by how many followers or likes you have, and the list goes on. We do the same thing in our moral behavior, but we don't measure our success off the Bible or Jesus because that's seemingly too out of reach, so basically we measure our success or goodness off other people. We measure our good deeds off other people, we measure our behavior off other people, and we even measure our sins or mistakes off other people. The issue with measurement is that it gives birth to an ugly set of twins, one is called 'comparison' the other is called 'judgment'. We compare and we judge others because it makes us feel better. Because "hey I might be screwed up but at least I'm not as screwed up as them." For a brief moment we find a sense of satisfaction, but like a snowflake in the palm of your hand, it dissipates quickly. It takes our attention off our insufficiency, but that's not good! It's in our insufficiency that grace is activated! Paul knew this all too well.

"...My grace is sufficient for you, for my power is made perfect in weakness." Therefore I will boast all the more gladly about my weaknesses, so that Christ's power may rest on me." (2 Corinthians 12:9)

Paul starts this letter to the Galatian church by declaring that his identity is based not on who man says he is, his own activity, performance or status among men:

"Paul, an apostle—sent not from men nor by a man, but by Jesus Christ and God the Father"

He simple says this, "Who I am by the grace of God, I didn't earn it, I didn't achieve it, it was a free gift. Even in my messed up state, God gave himself for me. His performance on the Cross eliminated my need to perform before man. The Cross eliminates my constant desire to find acceptance and approval from people or position. The security of my identity is found in Jesus' performance on my behalf through the Cross. What I love about this introduction that Paul writes to the Galatian church, is that Paul is being extremely intentional in declaring who he is. Before someone else tells him who he is. Before the world, your past, your social circle tells you who we are, we must establish who Christ has already made us.

Our identity is not determined by our issues, but the cause of our issues is our identity. One the biggest causes of insecurity, fear, anxiety and doubt comes from yours and my issue with our identity. Jesus wants us to know our identity is 'in him'. Our identity is not wrapped up in our activity. Our activity comes from first knowing our identity in Jesus.

So what happened on the Cross that so radically alters my identity?

1. Because of Jesus' work on the Cross you are not what you have done, you are what Jesus has done on your behalf.

2. Because of Jesus' work on the Cross I no longer work for acceptance, I work from acceptance.

3. Because of Jesus' work on the Cross my identity is secure once and for all and is not swayed or altered by what others say or think of me or even what I think of myself.

One of the great realities is the truth that Grace (my gifting, opportunities, my success in life) was not based on a position man gave me, but by my position in Jesus. I heard a wise preacher once say, "Don't be confident in your gifting, be confident in his choice."

A Christ like identity will produce Christ like activity. What was Jesus' activity? Declaring the good news of the gospel to a lost, hurt and broken humanity.

The activity of a strictly inclusive church or person starts first with the reality that each of us personally was strictly included by God through Jesus!

Because of Jesus you and I are loved and accepted by God, **we have nothing to prove!** And it's from that nothing to prove reality that our activity starts to flow. The activity of spreading the word is that we don't measure or judge humanity, but that they are strictly included by God and by his church just as we where because of Jesus!

In the 1992 Olympics a young man stepped up to the starting line of what would be a significant race in his career. His name was Derek Redmond. As the starting gun fired Derek was off and running. He was steaming ahead of his competitors and the thought of victory flashed through his mind, but that thought was quick to change. Just a Derek was a little over the half way mark a sharp pain went up his left leg, his ham string had torn, and Derek hit the ground. With pain in his body and tears in his eyes Derek picked himself up and proceeded to drag himself towards the finish line. Out of no-where a figure emerged onto the track running over to scoop up Derek in to his arms, it was Derek's father. For the remainder of the race Derek and his father clung together and slowly made their way towards the finish line. A report later revealed that all the way towards the finish line Derek's fathers kept repeating these words, "You're a champion son, you've got nothing to prove."

I love this story because it reminds us that our heavenly Father has done exactly that and more. Through Jesus' work on the Cross and the grace extended towards us, God has scooped us up in his arms and is journeying with us through the race of life, and repeating to us over and over again that because of Jesus 'We are champions and we have nothing to prove.'

Who are you? You are loved by God! You have nothing to prove, but you have a lot to show for it. Our activity is to show the world around us that they are loved by God - the same way he has loved us.

CHAPTER THREE

A Different Gospel

"I am astonished that you are so quickly deserting the one who called you to live in the grace of Christ and are turning to a different gospel— which is really no gospel at all. Evidently some people are throwing you into confusion and are trying to pervert the gospel of Christ. But even if we or an angel from heaven should preach a gospel other than the one we preached to you, let them be under God's curse! As we have already said, so now I say again: If anybody is preaching to you a gospel other than what you accepted, let them be under God's curse! Am I now trying to win the approval of human beings, or of God? Or am I trying to please people? If I were still trying to please people, I would not be a servant of Christ. (Galatians 1:6-10)

Getting married is amazing and one of the best things about getting married, besides playing monopoly whenever you want (hint hint monopoly is a code word), is the presents you receive on your wedding day! It's like a birthday party on steroids! And by far the best gift I received, the gift no man should ever be without, was the life changing gift of a 42inch plasma TV (keep in mind I got married in 2002 and they cost about $40,000 back then) I couldn't wait to get it set up in our new pad. We had this great little flat under a house over looking the beach in Sydney, but this house had one little problem that conflicted with my 42inch rectangle of glory....it had no aerial point. The only way we could set up the TV was to buy an old school Rabbit Ear antenna. I plugged it in and every time you changed the channel you had to change the position of the antenna rods. Sometimes I would even have to stand in a certain yoga pretzel like stance in order to maintain a decent picture.

One day a friend came over to watch the football (or the notebook) and he witnessed my frustration. He mentioned to me that this is a really easy problem to solve all I needed to do was to go down to the local shop and buy a HD digital set top box and if I did so not only will I get a picture, but I would get it in HIGH DEFINITION! I didn't even jump in the car, I ran like Forest Gump down to the local shop and pleaded for someone to tell me where I could find a HD digital set top box. A kind elderly lady employee pointed me to the correct aisle. So after holding her with a warm embrace I ran to the aisle. There it was a HD Digital set top box. I held it in the air like Simba in *The Lion King* "Nants ingonyama bagithi baba" (FYI that the actual words from *The Lion King* song), sure a little awkward and over the top, but it felt right! I rushed home plugged it in and it happened... a crystal clear high definition picture!

I think in the same way people have viewed the gospel like rabbit ear antennas, trying to establish a clear understanding of who God really is and what exactly does he think of me. Just when you think you've got a reasonably visible idea of God, someone or something comes and distorts it all over again. But God wants to make the picture crystal clear, he wants you and I to see the gospel in its simplest yet most powerful way. To see His love, demonstrated through Jesus' death, burial and resurrection in high definition.

In order to be a strictly inclusive church we must make clearer the message of the gospel.

Paul makes this crazy statement that the churches in Galatian are subscribing to a different gospel and not the clear simple one that they first heard, understood and believed. So what is a different gospel? Or how do you know if you have tuned into or are broadcasting a different gospel?

1. A different gospel tells you that you have to pay God back for what he did through Jesus.

Here is a confronting but liberating truth. God didn't save you because he had a hidden agenda of what he was going to get out of you once you accepted him. He didn't pay the ultimate price with an expectation that you would pay him back. Let me put it this way. Let's just say you had a gambling problem, I'm talking a really bad gambling problem, a few wins led to greed and you went all in but lost and you found yourself owing an overwhelming amount of debt $64 billion dollars!!!!! (I told you it was bad) and you needed to pay it back or it would cost your life. In your hast you run to the one thing that could help, a local coffee shop and just as you went into the coffee shop you bumped into a guy in the coffee line and you started chatting only to find that it wasn't any ordinary guy, it was the Bill Gates!

Its gets better! What started as an ordinary conversation quickly developed into a friendship, you confided in Bill and told him about your current predicament and your $64 billion dollar debt. Bill in his love and kindness decided that he was going to take care of your little (HUGE) debt. All $64 Billion dollars worth! And just as he signed over the amount, directly deposited it into your account you turned to him and declared "Billy G" (that's what his friends call him) "I promise I am going to pay you back, I'm going to pay back every dollar!"

How many people know that is a ridiculous statement and an impossible task. In the same way, to try and pay God back for the gift of salvation he gave is also ridiculous and impossible. I use this radical illustration to prove a radical point! You can never pay God back for what he has done for you.

A different gospel leaves you living with a sense of obligation towards God. He did all this so really I should do something for him. NO.

Now this is where I am starting to lose some church leaders,

A Different Gospel

but let me make something clear, does the grace of God cause me to sit around being a lazy lethargic Christian? NO, but our motivation to do things for God and with God in this life is not 'obligation' it's 'imitation'. Love's motivation is not 'well I guess I better because they love me' no it's 'I love because He first loved me and now I copy what he does, like a loving child imitating the father they love. Even Jesus said in John 8 that he just imitates the Father he loves.

Stop trying to pay God back, enjoy, and be grateful for the debt he paid on your behalf.

2. A different gospel tells you that now you have accepted Jesus 'I' better start changing myself and getting 'my' act together

It's amazing how when we come to Jesus it's all him but really soon after it's all back on us. Typical scenario; a young man who is addicted to drugs comes to church to hear the gospel. He hears that Jesus loves him even in his drug-addicted state and he gets so rocked that he says, "Yes I want to follow this Jesus who so loves me." They pray the prayer of salvation and the next morning they wake up with this flesh driven conclusion, 'I'm a Christian now and Christians behave a certain way so **I** better stop doing drugs and **I** should stop swearing and **I** will stop sleeping around every night and **I** need to reconcile my relationship with my parents,' and so forth. Before I go any further we must come to the conclusion that all these things are very wise things to do (but here comes my big but) BUT what is the common denominator in this equation? It's actually the same common denominator that got you into this whole mess... 'I.' 'I' better, 'I' should, 'I' will,'I' need....its all I,I,I.

If I got me into this mess, then what makes me think or trust that 'I' can get me out of this mess and make me a better person? You see we have a massive 'I' problem in the world today, even in the church. For some reason we think of Jesus as a one stop shop that we only have to visit once to pick up our salvation, but the rest of the journey is up to us to figure out. I use the word 'no' a lot in this book, maybe because I have twin toddlers who always grab everything sharp in our house, but once again I say to you NOOOOOOO. 'I' is not the answer. 'He' is and will always be the answer.

Christianity is not a religion based on behavioral modification; it's a relationship that daily trusts in Jesus' transforming power!

The reason why Paul said in Galatians 2:20 "..*it is no longer I who live, but Christ lives in me,*" is because he recognized that '*I*' just won't work anymore.

The same Jesus that you trusted to save you, is the same Jesus you need to trust to change you.

You will find that something inside of you, the Holy Spirit, will start to reveal things in you that He wants to heal, restore, and renew. But it's by His spirit and strength as you learn to rely and trust in him to work on you . The change Jesus also brings can come in the form of wisdom, friends, pastors, good council, but recognize it's from him!

I was at the snow once and the day we arrived there was a crazy snow-storm that went on through the night. The next morning I woke up to look out the window and see a beautiful, strangely hot and blue sky day. I looked at the trees covered, weighed down and buried in snow. I noticed, as the sun grew higher in the sky that day, the snow just started to drip and fall off the trees. Sometimes the snow would come crashing off in huge portions. Did the trees try to shake or scrap the snow from their branches? No. It was simply the exposure to the sun that lifted the burden of the snow off the trees. My point. Keep exposing yourself to Jesus, the Son, trusting and seeking him, and the change that you need will just happen. A different gospel makes it all about you and 'I', but a strictly inclusive gospel, or the real gospel makes it all about Him.

3. A differing gospel says you haven't pleased God yet.

I think one of the biggest issues we all face is the need to want to please people. It's almost as if the affirmation and acceptance of others has become an oxygen we suck into the lungs of our identity and exhale a sense of worth from it. Pleasing others becomes a motivator, it drives us and almost becomes like a drug that we need our fix from and if we don't get it we fall apart. Imagine what it would feel like to not care what people think? To live happily with who you are in Christ, to live with confidence and boldness! Let me hit you with some life changing knowledge…once you accepted Jesus and his grace YOU BECAME PLEASING TO GOD. I will say it again YOU PLEASE GOD! God is happy with you! God is pumped with you, excited about you, proud of you! Wait a minute I didn't do anything? Exactly JESUS DID IT ALL!

There is a beautiful event that takes place during Jesus' crucifixion *(Luke 23:26-43)*. Jesus was crucified between two thieves, they both deserved to be on their cross. One thief mocks Jesus, while the other does the complete opposite, he admits he deserves his punishment and death, but he asks Jesus to remember him in paradise. Jesus says some of the most beautiful life giving words, *"Today you will be with me in Paradise."* Stop the press!! Hold on, he didn't do anything! The thief didn't have time to serve in a church, help the homeless, attend a church conference, sponsor a child, bring a friend to church, lift his hands in worship. Again none of these things are wrong, there are beautiful and Christ like, but in that moment Jesus proves something to all of us through his act of mercy to the thief on the other cross. It is Jesus action of sacrifice, mercy and forgiveness poured out on the cross that makes us pleasing to God. It has nothing to do with us. This thief's passport to paradise was based on Christ performance not his own.

When Jesus was pinned to that cross, the cross we deserved, the weight of all the things that didn't please God in our lives where placed onto him. Through his love and sacrifice we went in reeking to high heaven of sin, shame, and filth, but came out the other side smelling like a rose. When Jesus said those powerful final words on the cross "IT IS FINISHED", the end of performance driven acceptance came to a crashing end! We no longer need to strive to please God or men. Jesus finished it that day on the cross. YOU PLEASE GOD!

The devil knows that when it comes to your right standing and approval status with God, it is finished, and he hates that! So being the great deceiver that he is, he slithers along into the minds and hearts of believers and tells them to keep trying because you don't please God yet. On top of that some religious beliefs also subscribe to this lie and try to place expectations and requirements on believers that urge them to keep trying to please God by their performance and efforts. The danger of this is what they are saying is Jesus' death on the death cross wasn't enough! That he wasn't the perfect sacrifice and that there is still more to be done to please God. That my friends, is not the real gospel, that is a different gospel that you should reject. Because of Jesus, YOU PLEASE GOD!

Even Jesus didn't work to get approval. In Matthew 3:13-17, Jesus came to be baptized from John the Baptist. When he came up out of the water a voice declared, "This is my son, whom I love, in him I am well pleased." But wait a second, he hadn't started his ministry yet, he hadn't done anything!!! In the same way we where baptized into Jesus and now God declares over you and me, "This is my child, whom I love, In them I am well pleased!"

I don't work **to** receive a place of approval; I work **from** a place of approval.

It is from this place that we live and move and have our being. Yes we labor and advance the message of the gospel, but it is from the deeply secure place of my approval in God. He is pleased with you!

A strictly inclusive gospel although pleasing is never aimed at pleasing men, it will unsettle the religious and performance driven people because it takes the attention off them. The true gospel puts all the attention on Jesus.

A different gospel distorts the truth and the radical nature of a strictly inclusive gospel. Its makes it all about man's ways, efforts and abilities, it throws people into chaos and confusion.

The true gospel, or the truth in high definition, makes an extremely clear picture; it is all about Jesus, what he did for us and what he will do in us and through us.

CHAPTER FOUR

A Revelation, A Reminder and A Rejoice

"I want you to know, brothers and sisters, that the gospel I preached is not of human origin. I did not receive it from any man, nor was I taught it; rather, I received it by revelation from Jesus Christ. For you have heard of my previous way of life in Judaism, how intensely I persecuted the church of God and tried to destroy it. 14 I was advancing in Judaism beyond many of my own age among my people and was extremely zealous for the traditions of my fathers. 15 But when God, who set me apart from my mother's womb and called me by his grace, was pleased to reveal his Son in me so that I might preach him among the Gentiles, my immediate response was not to consult any human being. I did not go up to Jerusalem to see those who were apostles before I was, but I went into Arabia. Later I returned to Damascus. Then after three years, I went up to Jerusalem to get acquainted with Cephas[a] and stayed with him fifteen days. 19 I saw none of the other apostles—only James, the Lord's brother. I assure you before God that what I am writing you is no lie. Then I went to Syria and Cilicia. 22 I was personally unknown to the churches of Judea that are in Christ. They only heard the report: "The man who formerly persecuted us is now preaching the faith he once tried to destroy." And they praised God because of me. (Galatians 1:11-24)

W̲hen did Santa Claus begin? We all know that only God is eternal. So how did this wonderful Christmas character begin? We didn't make him up. Saint Nicholas, whose name was changed over the years to Santa Claus, was a real person, a bishop in the church in the fourth century.

In Saint Nicholas' time, a young woman had to have a dowry (money or material things which she brought to her husband) before she could be married. Saint Nicholas wanted to help a poor nobleman with three daughters, but he wanted to do it anonymously (without anyone knowing who did it). He didn't want to be praised for his generosity. He gave for the joy of giving. So, three bags of gold were thrown through the nobleman's window. However, the nobleman found out who had given the gold for his daughters' dowries. After that, anonymous gifts of charity often were attributed to Saint Nicholas. Or Santa Claus. And that's where it all began! Crazy huh!

So here is my point, how do we know that Jesus wasn't like old Saint Nick? Jesus was a good person who did a lot of great things for people, so how do we know that his story was just a bunch of people who had a great affinity for a lovely kind Jewish carpenter who lived 2000ish years ago? (Straight away some of you are thinking, wow this guy isn't a very good Christian, he is making me question my faith?) No I am not here to make you question your faith but affirm your faith. What I have encountered in my years interacting with other fellow Christians is that most people are living on what I call a second hand faith, or a hand me down revelation of God. To be a strictly inclusive church we can't live on knowledge alone, because if someone can talk you into Jesus, than someone can talk you out of Jesus. It has to be deeper than that; it has to be more real than that!

Paul's point in this section of the letter to the Galatians is basically him saying, "Hey guys I didn't make this up, this wasn't just a half truth that snow balled into a big truth, this is real!"

Paul divulges these three powerful points that really act as a limpness test for our faith and belief in Jesus.

1. A Revelation

Paul says, "I didn't make this thing up, but it came to me by revelation." The word revelation means a striking disclosure. It is not just something that is revealed to you, it catches your attention and changes your view and understanding forever. Let me ask you this question: Do you know what happened when Jesus saved you? Let me use this story to illustrate my point.

On August 5th, 2010 most of us would have woke up to the news of a tragic mine collapse in Chili. Thirty three minors where trapped 2050 feet under ground with absolutely no way of getting themselves out. The local government and other professionals banned together to plan a way to rescue these men from this seemingly impossible situation. A long amazing story cut short - but a tunnel and lift shaft were built to pierce through the rock down to the men and after 69 days of these men being trapped they each came to the surface to breath fresh air, the rescue was a success.

Do you realize that in the same way we where trapped in our sin? Trapped in our shame? Trapped in an impossible situation that we could never get ourselves out of. But Jesus through the cross, made a way. Like a tunnel dug through 2050 feet of dirt, and by his grace lifted us back to life.

You see a revelation isn't that I believe there is a God now. A revelation is I realize I was trapped in my sin, in an impossible situation and no amount of good works or efforts could dig my way out of this. I was as good as dead! But Jesus came after me!! Why is the understanding of my state without God and his grace so important? Truth is the grace of God only really becomes amazing when you realize the mess you where in.

There is a story in *Luke 7:36-50* of a prostitute with perfume who bursts into a dinner party that a religious leader is holding for Jesus. She then pours perfume on his feet and proceeds to cry on his feet and then starts to wipe his feet with her hair. Everyone is shocked and appalled except for Jesus. He starts telling a story of two people who are in debt to a money-lender. One owes $50 the other $500, they both can't pay, so the money lender cancels both of their debts. Jesus asks the religious leaders, based on this act of mercy, who will love the money-lender more? Then Simon the religious leader answers correctly and concludes it would be the one who owed the most? Jesus then affirms his answer. He then goes onto say something that has always rattled me in verse 47:

"Therefore I tell you, her many sins have been forgiven – as her great love has shown. But whoever has been forgiven little loves little."

I have to be honest with you, when I first read this I was a little disheartened. I thought to myself, 'Well, I've never been a prostitute (don't be shocked), I've never taken cocaine, I've never done anything really that bad, so does that mean my love for Jesus won't be as great as someone who gone through those things? I haven't been forgiven as much as others because my past hasn't been that extreme?' Then it hit me, Jesus wasn't just trying to prove a point of mercy to the prostitute; he was trying to show a truth to the religious leaders. The truth being that the reason why Simon didn't find grace that amazing and didn't love as much is because he still thought he was good. He thought he wasn't as bad as the prostitute with the perfume. Truth is we are all sinners trapped and incapable of escaping; there is no difference between a prostitute's sin and a priest's sin. Sin is sin. We are all beggars in debt, but Jesus by his grace wipes the slate clean. Do you want your love for Christ to increase? Reflect on how much you where in debt and how much he rescued you from. The more I reflect on how far gone I was the more amazing his grace gets and the more my love for him increases. You love much when you realize how much you have been forgiven.

The beauty is, he has a desire to do the same for all humanity. I can't be satisfied that I made it out alive. I have to tell others. The truth is everyone's tunnel has already been dug; Jesus' work on the cross was once and for all. It is our job to shout down the tunnel of people's lives and to encourage them to hop into the lift of God's grace and come to the surface to breathe the fresh air of his love, mercy, forgiveness and freedom. Now that's a revelation that will change your world forever!

2. A Reminder

On just about every car there is a huge windscreen to look through, but also a small review mirror to occasionally look back into. In the same way God wants us to look forward into the glorious future he has planned for us, like Paul says in Phillipians 3:13 "... *forgetting what is behind and straining toward what is ahead..*" so our intention is to look ahead! As much as there is a need to look forward there is also a time to look back. Not to look back on past mistakes, failures and sins, but look back and to see what God rescued you out of! You see as you move forward you will hit obstacles and road-blocks in your life. It is in that time that we need to look back and remember what Christ did for us when he rescued and redeemed us. I'm amazed at how often Paul the apostle wrote to remind people of their status and state with God. He constantly wrote to remind us of what exactly happened when they accepted Christ as their savior. In Colossians 3:1-3, Paul pens these amazing words through the inspiration of the Holy Spirit to remind us what took place:

"Since, then, you have been raised with Christ, set your hearts on things above, where Christ is, seated at the right hand of God. 2 Set your minds on things above, not on earthly things. 3 For you died, and your life is now hidden with Christ in God." (Colossians 3:1-3)

Paul declares some amazing truths in just these few short versus. Let's break down exactly what happened.

A. You Died

Paul brings across this seemingly morbid point that we died! Wait a second Paul I'm pretty sure I'm still kicking and breathing, so what is Paul trying to say? When we made the decision to say 'yes' to Jesus we attended our own funeral. What died was your previous way of life, your sin, shame, guilt, fear, insecurities, all the things that you and I are ashamed of. It all was attached to you and the only way to get rid of it was for you to die in your previous way of life, your old nature. Let me paint a picture for you that helped me. Imagine an open coffin, and now see yourself throwing boxes into that coffin. The boxes have words written on them, one box says SHAME and all the things in your life that you are ashamed of are in that box and you're throwing it into that coffin. Now see a box and written on it is the word FEAR, inside that box are all the things that your fearful of, fear of rejection, fear of failure, fear of people, fear of the future, it's all in that fear box and now that box is being thrown into the coffin. Along with all the other boxes that represent the insufficiencies, faults and messes in our lives! Now see that coffin being nailed shut, but it's not being taken out to be buried in the grave yard of our subconscious. NO it's going to be cremated by the red hot flames of God's Love, mercy and Grace. You and your old life died!

Let me ask you this, have you ever been to a funeral and in the middle of the solemn ceremony a stranger comes bursting into the church and runs towards the coffin and starts yelling, accusing, blaming, ranting and raving at the dead person in the coffin, 'You're a loser, you're worthless, your guilty of this and that, you owe me, and so forth ????' I am almost 100% sure that no one has ever experienced this. Why? Because there is no point accusing a dead person!! When the devil, who is the accuser of the brethren, comes to accuse us for the faults and failures in our lives, what he finds is a dead person in whom he can bring no accusation. There are some people who need a strong reminder right now as you read this. To remind the accuser, sorry devil I died, that's not who I am any more; I am a new creation in Christ Jesus!!!! Renew your mind everyday and remind yourself the same as Paul did in Galatians 2:20, *"Its no longer I who live but Christ who lives in me"* COME ON!! THAT'S A LIFE CHANGING POWERFUL TRUTH TO BE REMINDED OF!!

B. *You are Hidden*

Not only are you dead, which is an amazing powerful reality, God takes it one step further. He hides you! Imagine you are holding a pen and someone came along and they really wanted that pen, so they try and fight you for it. You might be a strong person and maybe able to handle your own, but now I want you to image yourself giving that pen to the biggest most strongest person you can think of (like a mister universe or UFC heavy weight champion). They put it in their pocket. If that same person wants the pen, they don't have to fight you, they have to fight them. The odds have dramatically changed!! Let's now change that pen and replace it with you, and that stranger who wants you, is the devil. You, like the pen, are now in the hands of literally Mr. Universe himself JESUS and he has hidden you in his pocket. If the devil wants to get you he has to go through Jesus. The fight was over before it even began! You're hidden in Christ.

Lets go deeper, if the devil comes to bring accusation, blame and guilt against you, when he goes to find you all he keeps seeing is Jesus! Spotless, blameless, sin conquering Jesus. The devil doesn't stand a chance!

It's easy to become a strictly inclusive person and church when we realize where we came from. It had nothing to do with us; it had everything to do with a loving heroic savior. It's from that place that we share the good news that Jesus can do the same for anyone!

We all need to look back in the rearview mirror of our lives and remind ourselves of what Jesus did for us.

3. A Rejoice

What I love about this final point that Paul brings up is that the church should always be a place of rejoicing. He's not just talking about praise and worship in our services or gatherings.

He is talking about a rejoicing that comes when we celebrate the lives that Jesus has changed. Paul was a bad dude who was guilty of destroying churches, families and lives, but when he meets Jesus and the word spreads to the same churches he was trying to destroy, they REJOICED. I don't know about you but sometimes I've noticed the rejoicing of our changed lives. Ever observed someone coming to Christ and they are so pumped, I'm talking four cans of Red Bull pumped, they bring friends left, right and center, they serve with zeal, they pray with passion, but the more they hang out with the more accustomed believers its like that fire and passions seems to die. I know I've been guilty of that. Why does this happen? I believe it's because we have forgotten the revelation of what Jesus rescued us from. We need a reminder of what he did for us on the cross and in turn we will find rejoicing springing up from within us as we spectate and celebrate that same thing happen for others.

A Strictly inclusive church will always have reason to rejoice because it's more focused on the reaching of the lost than the comfort of the saints. The side effect will be humanity pouring into church, receiving Jesus, and that is always going to be a party!

Maybe take some time right now to reflect on the revelation of where Jesus brought you from, a reminder of what the repercussions of the cross means for you and rejoice that he did and can, and will do it for others.

CHAPTER FIVE

The Toy Lawnmower

(A STRICTLY INCLUSIVE CHURCH
IS ALWAYS EVANGELISTIC)

"Then after fourteen years, I went up again to Jerusalem, this time with Barnabas. I took Titus along also. I went in response to a revelation and, meeting privately with those esteemed as leaders, I presented to them the gospel that I preach among the Gentiles. I wanted to be sure I was not running and had not been running my race in vain. Yet not even Titus, who was with me, was compelled to be circumcised, even though he was a Greek. This matter arose because some false believers had infiltrated our ranks to spy on the freedom we have in Christ Jesus and to make us slaves. We did not give in to them for a moment, so that the truth of the gospel might be preserved for you. As for those who were held in high esteem— whatever they were makes no difference to me; God does not show favoritism—they added nothing to my message. On the contrary, they recognized that I had been entrusted with the task of preaching the gospel to the uncircumcised, just as Peter had been to the circumcised. For God, who was at work in Peter as an apostle to the circumcised, was also at work in me as an apostle to the Gentiles. James, Cephas[c] and John, those esteemed as pillars, gave me and Barnabas the right hand of fellowship when they recognized the grace given to me. They agreed that we should go to the Gentiles, and they to the circumcised. All they asked was that we should continue to remember the poor, the very thing I had been eager to do all along. (Galatians 2:1-10)

In the early years of our marriage my wife Alanna and I rented a little granny flat on the edge of cliff over looking a beautiful picturesque beach.

It was amazing except for one little problem, it had a lawn. Now there is nothing wrong with having a lawn, except for the painful task of having to mow it! Yep you guessed it, I hate mowing. So stinking boring and if I had it my way I would get one of those plastic look alike lawns (don't judge me). Nevertheless every couple of weeks I would begrudgingly mow the lawn. My son Bailey was nearly 2 years old at this point and every time I would mow the lawn and he would walk over to the back glass door and smudge his cute little face against the glass absolutely bamboozled. I could only imagine what his little brain was thinking, 'oh my gosh, that thing eats grass!'

Not long after its was Bailey's second birthday and his great grandmother bought him a little toy lawn mower, it had a little handle you could pull that made the sound of a little lawn mower, it was awesome. I used to play with it when he was sleeping (again, don't judge). Soon the time came for me to mow the lawns... again! I got out the lawn mower and wheeled it to the back yard and as I reached down to pull the start up cord, a tiny little figure was standing right next to me. My boy Bailey, also with a lawn mower, his tiny toy lawn mower. I reached down to pull the cord, he reached down to pull the cord, I pushed the mower up the grass, he followed pushing the lawn mower right next to me. Everything I did, he did. (I know right? super cute, don't hold back the tears, let them flow, its natural). Now let me tell you what didn't happen, my wife Alanna and I didn't sit down with him on his second birthday and explain to him that now he was two he needed to start contributing around the house more. That he can't just sit around free loading, eating our food, sleeping under our roof, he needed to get to work! That conversation, although enticing, never happened. **All my son was doing was imitating the father he loved!**

You see the heart of evangelism is not obligation, but imitation. We are simply imitating what we have first seen the father do. Paul is basically saying in this passage of Galatians, that the preaching of the gospel and the reaching of the lost, the down and out is not something he feels obligated to do. He says I'm doing this in response to a revelation. God had showed him love, grace and mercy and from that came a love response! ***Christianity is not an action, but a re-action***. We are simply responding to what God first did for us.

The heart, the purpose and the action of a strictly inclusive church is devoted to loving Jesus and a passionate response is to reaching those far from God.

Here are four motivators of a strictly inclusive church.

1. The Mandate

It wasn't the great suggestion but the great commission. We exist to reach those who are far from God. I love 2 Corinthians 5:14-19: ***"For Christ's love compels us, because we are convinced that one died for all, and therefore all died. And he died for all, that those who live should no longer live for themselves but for him who died for them and was raised again. So from now on we regard no one from a worldly point of view. Though we once regarded Christ in this way, we do so no longer. Therefore, if anyone is in Christ, the new creation has come: The old has gone, the new is here! All this is from God, who reconciled us to himself through Christ and gave us the ministry of reconciliation: that God was reconciling the world to himself in Christ, not counting people's sins against them. And he has committed to us the message of reconciliation.***

Based on the mandate that is the ministry of reconciliation here are a few things we don't do:

A) We are not selective in who can come into our community – we have been convinced Christ died for all. We are strictly Inclusive because Christ died to make it that way.

B) We don't live for ourselves – Jesus died and made it all about me so I don't have to live for me anymore.

C) We don't judge people from a worldly perspective – the world judges and labels people by there activity, we don't. We see the gold in the dirt.

D) We don't count sins – what you can count you can measure and what you can measure you can judge. So we've stopped counting, which means we stop judging and focus more on caring.

2. The Method

The Jewish church leaders represented here in the book of Galatians were all about methods that you took part in to get yourself closer to God. Methods became so sacred that the message was lost. A strictly inclusive church clings with white knuckles to the message and holds very loosely the methods. A strictly inclusive church will do just about anything to see people come to Christ. Extreme? Absolutely! Jesus broke the methods to reinforce the message. You are loved by God! Don't be precious with the methods, but rather be precious with the message and be precious with the people Jesus died to reach.

3. The Meaning

The meaning of the message will cause you to get your hands dirty. The meaning will force you and I not to get stuck in a Christian bubble. It will cause you to reject the monastery mentality that separates the church from the world. This is to avoid being infected with the un-holiness of the world around us. But instead it plunge's you into the darkest of places in order to shine the light of his grace and mercy. The meaning will motivate you to see the saint behind the sinner. The meaning will make you persevere with patience when dealing with the down and out. Ultimately the meaning will make you more Christ like. What is the meaning? Christ Jesus came into the world to save sinners!!!

Remember we where there once too. So despite popular opinion we can relate with a sinful world because we used to live in it. The meaning motivates me to become a paramedic on the battlefield of sin. Finding people and putting them on the stretcher of compassion and patience and carrying them to the master soul physician, Jesus!

4. The Men

One of the things, among many, that blows my mind about God and his radical rescue plan for humanity is the fact that he uses men or people to do it! The overwhelming reality that an all-powerful God would include us in his redemption plan is astounding! Now before you disqualify yourself and think that your not the type of person God would use, let me interject. Paul was once called Saul. Saul was a bad man, so bad that he was responsible for the death of many Christian people. If anyone could have an excuse to disqualify themselves it was Paul. I have taken up way too much mental real estate with thoughts and reasons of why God wouldn't or shouldn't choose me or use me, but check out what Paul writes to the church in Colosse and makes plain a radical truth: ***"...and giving joyful thanks to the Father, who has qualified you to share in the inheritance of his holy people in the kingdom of light."*** (Colossians 1:12)

Did you catch that? HE HAS QUALIFIED YOU!! When it came to selecting a player for his team you weren't the last to be picked, he chose you! But not only did he choose you, he qualified you. So here is my big point, '**Don't be confident in your gifting, be confident in his choice**.' You may have heard this before, but this statement is true. God doesn't call the qualified, he qualifies the called! The other side of this is that Paul doesn't need man's motivation to do what he knows God has called him to do. Yes he was a man under authority but he wasn't a man under the persuasion of his peers. To be a strictly inclusive church won't always be a popular thing, self righteous, religious people won't approve of it. So you need to know you are called to reach the lost, which we all are called to do, and be confident in the relentless grace and mercy that God has called us to be advocates of.

We must understand that the church has been graced, empowered and equipped to reach the lost and make disciples for Jesus. A strictly inclusive church does not have an evangelistic month every year to try and re-ignite the congregation's passion for the lost. It's evangelistic 12 months of the year. We exist to pursue Jesus and pursue the lost. My pastor, Ps Phil Pringle, says this:

"When everyone is catching fish everyone is happy, but when no one is catching fish, we turn on each other."

A great way to create more pastoral issues and build a myopic culture in our churches is take our foot off the accelerator of evangelism. I hear a lot of people say our job is to help people mature in their faith and that is true, but one of the quickest ways to mature a person in their faith is for them to reach people with the message of the gospel. The quickest way to create joy and excitement in our churches is to have people responding to the gospel every week in our gatherings. A strictly inclusive church is not seasonally evangelistic; its annual mission is the reaching of those far from God.

CHAPTER SIX

Room At The Table

"When Cephas came to Antioch, I opposed him to his face, because he stood condemned. For before certain men came from James, he used to eat with the Gentiles. But when they arrived, he began to draw back and separate himself from the Gentiles because he was afraid of those who belonged to the circumcision group. The other Jews joined him in his hypocrisy, so that by their hypocrisy even Barnabas was led astray. When I saw that they were not acting in line with the truth of the gospel, I said to Cephas in front of them all, "You are a Jew, yet you live like a Gentile and not like a Jew. How is it, then, that you force Gentiles to follow Jewish customs? "We who are Jews by birth and not sinful Gentiles know that a person is not justified by the works of the law, but by faith in Jesus Christ. So we, too, have put our faith in Christ Jesus that we may be justified by faith in[a] Christ and not by the works of the law, because by the works of the law no one will be justified. "But if, in seeking to be justified in Christ, we Jews find ourselves also among the sinners, doesn't that mean that Christ promotes sin? Absolutely not! If I rebuild what I destroyed, then I really would be a lawbreaker. "For through the law I died to the law so that I might live for God. I have been crucified with Christ and I no longer live, but Christ lives in me. The life I now live in the body, I live by faith in the Son of God, who loved me and gave himself for me. I do not set aside the grace of God, for if righteousness could be gained through the law, Christ died for nothing!" (Galatians 2:11-21)

I think one of the scariest moments in young man's life. The first time you go over to your girlfriend's parents house for dinner. My wife Alanna and I started dating when we where 16 years old and a few months into our courtship it was time to venture into the mysterious world of the unknown girlfriend's house (or potential in-laws). When you arrive you have a thousand thoughts running through your head, 'don't talk too much, make eye contact, shake her Dad's hand firmly, but not too strong let him know you're strong but you respect him as the alpha male in the house, and last but not least, don't be a loser'. I am pretty sure I failed all of these. We were about to sit down for dinner, but nature was calling so I quickly excused myself to go to the bathroom. When I went to wash my hands the unthinkable happened. I turned on the tap and the water came rushing out like a high- pressure hose and splashed all over the front of my grey colored pants!!! My first thought was maybe I could convince them that peeing your pants is the coolest, and that everyone is doing it these days? Nah. I quickly grabbed the hand towel and began to sponge my pants, but the watermark would not relent. I knew I couldn't stay in there too long or they would think I had a bowel problem. So I concluded that if I could just make it back to the table and quickly sit down, the extended dinner would allow my predicament to dry up. I left the bathroom facing the wall and clung to it like Silvester Stalonne in the movie Cliffhanger. I pretended to look at all the photos whilst making random comments about how amazing everyone looked and how I loved old pictures (liar) I followed the perimeter of wall around to the table and rushed to my sit. Mission accomplished. Awkward moment avoided.

I am amazed at how many people see the table of fellowship that is the church just like this. I think I'm welcome at the table, but not too sure if I can come like this? I need to cautiously make my way hiding my mess from other people, by distracting people with my wit and personality, my smiling face and good manners, anything to take the attention off them seeing who I really am. Isn't that the case sometimes with all of us? We use our serving or our passionate worship, or bubbly personalities to distract people from who we really are. Why do we do that? Simple. We all long for acceptance. If I'm not appealing or acceptable, well the conclusion we arrive at is that I won't fit in here. I won't be accepted, there won't be room at the table for me, so we fake it until we make it to the table. The truth is regardless of your mess, THERE IS ROOM AT THE TABLE FOR YOU, in fact there is room for everybody.

Let us examine ourselves and our churches with these two questions:

1. Do you know you're welcome at the table of Lord?

2. Are you making others welcome at the table of fellowship?

In this passage of Galatians there is a dinner party going down and Peter the head of the church is there, hanging with the Gentiles, the outcasts, the riffraff, and is having a jolly good time. But suddenly another group arrive at the dinner party, the Jewish gang (the legalistic mob) enter the room. Peter who usually rolls with the Jewish gang suddenly pulls back from the table and casually pretends like he didn't know how he got to the dinner party and that he doesn't even like the people in the room. Hold on a second! This is Peter, the rock, the one Jesus put in charge to run the church, what is he doing? Let's pause for a second and take a slight tangent from our topic at hand to remind ourselves of this: There is no such thing as a perfect leader or pastor, we all make mistakes, so don't put your hope in a person or you're going to get let down I can guarantee it, put your hope in Jesus and you will never be disappointed.

So why did Peter pull back from the table, why did he become strictly EX-clusive?

Fear. Fear of what other people would think of him. Peter was so consumed with the approval of others that it caused him to ignore the gospel of grace for the sake of acceptance. If we honestly search our lives we have all encountered these moments. We receive grace freely but we withhold it from others, because if we get too crazy with this accepting inclusive grace it may cause us to lose some prominence and position with the so called 'popular crowd'. Maybe even the popular church crowd. The powerful response of the gospel is that it will compel us to accept the rejected, embrace the awkward, and eat with the unpopular.

So what can help me overcome my fear of men and embrace the unpopular? Here it is. God invited and allowed you to sit at his table. Regardless of your state he embraced you. So here are a few things that will cause you to make room at your table of fellowship:

1. God made room for you

We weren't invited to the table because we were popular, because we attracted the attention of God with our goodness, or that he wanted to glean from our coolness. NOPE. We where not invited by merit, we where invited by Grace. As Mark Twain puts it:

> "IF HEAVEN WENT BY MERIT, OUR DOG WOULD
> GET IN, AND WE WOULD BE KICKED OUT."

God allowed us to come and sit in fellowship with him even though we where dressed in sin, stinking garments and even our prideful posture. He welcomed us. If I didn't get there of my own accord, why would I impose that requirement on others? Isn't it funny that people who were not invited to the grace party, now stand at the door stopping other uninvited people from coming in. It's backwards! None of us were on the 'VIP List', we were the 'not a chancers', the rejects, on the black list, but Jesus let us come to the party, with hope we would include others.

Early twentieth century Baptist minister Oswald Chambers made this beautiful statement regarding the heart behind extending grace to people:

> "I HAVE NEVER MET THE MAN I COULD
> DESPAIR OF AFTER DISCERNING WHAT LIES IN
> ME APART FROM THE GRACE OF GOD."

This is what Paul is trying to get across in his seemingly aggressive conversation with Peter. He was simply saying "Hey Pete, remember how you didn't earn this? Remember how this was a free gift, paid for at the expense of Christ on the cross? Remember how he made room for you, so you should also make room for others?" Remember what lies in you apart from the grace of God.

Apart from the grace of God, we are no more deserving than the next person. I think we need to remind ourselves frequently of the life we lived before we sat at the table, not in a self-defeating way, but in a sobering way. He made room so we can also make room for others.

2. Receive his Perfect Love

We all have fears, but one of the biggest fears we face is the fear of other people's opinions. It will paralyze you from your freedom. It will confuse your identity and take away your liberty in Christ. To live driven by the opinions of others, is to never truly live at all. You are like a puppet on a string whose every move is not your own, but under the dictatorship of the thoughts and opinions of others. Have you been there? I know I have. It's the chronic illness of 'People Pleasing'. You don't do what you want to do, you just do what you think will please others. People Pleasing is a debilitating disease. Instead of walking by faith you are carried off in the crowd, the parade of the seemingly popular. Peter was just like us and suffered the same illness. We really can't be too hard on Peter because we have all been there and done that. So how do I get out of it? How do I conquer it? Once upon a time I would have said, 'Greater Faith', if I had greater faith I could withstand the temptation to please people, but that's not it. Check this out:

"There is no fear in love. But perfect love drives out fear, because fear has to do with punishment. The one who fears is not made perfect in love." (1 John 4:18)

There it is! The answer to all fear and especially to the fear of the opinion of people is **perfect love.** We need to meditate on God's perfect love for us.

C.S. Lewis put it this way:

> "On the whole, God's love for us
> is a much safer subject to think
> about than our love for Him."

God's love is not passive - it's aggressive. It comes into the heart and the mind like a relentless Navy Seal team and it drives out and destroys all fear... not some fear... ALL FEAR. God does not share space. He is all consuming, and so is his love, because he is Love!

To be a strictly inclusive church we must pay more attention to God's love and give less attention to our effort to love him. Why? Because our pursuit and endeavor to love God can cause us to take our attention off what God loves... People. Don't get me wrong we worship and show adoration to God, but let's not get so consumed with our love for God, that it takes our focus off what God loves. Perfect love is one-way love, it has no hidden agenda, it doesn't have time to think about itself; it is the gift that keeps on giving. Cancel out fear by allowing God's perfect love to impact you and work through you. You won't have time to fear, just to love. You won't live to please people, you'll live to love people and there is a big difference.

So what keeps people from the table of fellowship?

I think it is one thing to have a heart and a passion to invite people to the table, but I think it's also a great question to ask what keeps people from the table of fellowship?

1. Comparison – Manufactured self esteem

I think one of the biggest things that people who have never been in church find unusual and unattractive about the church is the comparison game we play. By nature we use our successes or failures to measure how good or bad we are. The problem with comparison is that it will cause you to live on a roller coaster of emotion. Up when you've done good, then down when you've done bad! Up when you're better than them, down when their better than you! Even worse than that we measure our goodness against people's badness in order to make ourselves feel better. Jesus tells this story:

"To some who were confident of their own righteousness and looked down on everyone else, Jesus told this parable: "Two men went up to the temple to pray, one a Pharisee and the other a tax collector. The Pharisee stood by himself and prayed: 'God, I thank you that I am not like other people—robbers, evildoers, adulterers—or even like this tax collector. I fast twice a week and give a tenth of all I get.' "But the tax collector stood at a distance. He would not even look up to heaven, but beat his breast and said, 'God, have mercy on me, a sinner.' "I tell you that this man, rather than the other, went home justified before God. For all those who exalt themselves will be humbled, and those who humble themselves will be exalted." (Luke 18:9-14)

The Pharisee had a massive comparison problem. He was so consumed with himself and his goodness he didn't even want to give attention to the broken man right beside him. When he did it was to measure himself off him. What is comparison? It is manufactured self-esteem. It's using other people to make yourself feel better. When people come into the church who haven't necessarily got there lives together, we look down on them from our self-righteous high horse. How do we think that makes them feel? Because they notice, they feel the vibe so to speak. A comparison driven person is a selfish person, because it causes you to be focused on your performance and prominence, it doesn't have time to love others. When we are driven by comparison we don't have time to make room at the table for others and we tell the world that we don't have time for them.

2. Legalism – preaching preference over truth

This is a big issue in the church today. Legalism is man having a personal preference and then turning that personal preference into gospel truth. Legalism is man creating personal rule in which someone must adhere to if they want a relationship with God.

Here is a great example of legalism in church life. A pastor or church leader might not like smoking and prefers not to smoke, and that's fine, it's your preference. But then one Sunday he gets up and declares, "Jesus doesn't like smoking, cigarettes are the devil's sticks, in fact if you smoke you're in danger of entering into an eternity of darkness and forced to eat cigarette sandwiches forever!" I know that sounds extreme, but there are churches that have preached similar messages.

Here's my point - there is nowhere in the Bible that condemns smoking. Is it bad for you? Yes. Can it kill you? Absolutely. However, the choice to smoke or not smoke is up to you. **It is your preference,** but you cannot make that preference gospel truth because it's not in the Bible. Some would say the Bible says, 'Your body is a temple of the Lord and you should take care of it, that's why you shouldn't smoke', and yes that true. But a smoke filled temple does not turn God away, and he will deal with it and renovate it in his good time. You worry about him working in your temple, and let Him work on theirs, but don't preach preference that tells people that God can't handle vices and addictions, when quite the opposite is true.

Legalism forces people to conform to a man made preference rather than be transformed by gospel truth. What has kept people away from the church for so long is that they heard people preach preference, the must do this, and the must do that. Do you know once upon a time preachers would preach against

'Rock'n'Roll' music, declaring it was the devil's music, drums are like witchcraft, amplified music is the devil. Why? The church at that time preferred its own style of music, another perfect case of preference rather than truth. The church majored on legalistic minors for so long that now when the major truths come up, no one wants to hear it. Let us focus on telling people the truth, and keep our preference to ourselves.

3. Hypocrisy – engage in the same behaviors you condemn.

I have often heard people say, "I don't like the church, it's full of hypocrites and I have to agree and at the same time disagree with that statement. Yes I agree the church is full of hypocrites because it is full of people. It's not just the church that is full of hypocrites, your local mall is full of hypocrites, your soccer team is full of hypocrites, your gym is full of hypocrites, your own house is full of hypocrites; all human beings are hypocrites. What really puts people off church the most is people who engage in the same behaviors they condemn. People who look down on people who drink alcohol, but then go out for a drink after church when no one is looking, or people who say they love people and speak well of them, but then reject people and bring people down with other believers in moments of gossip. People who say not to watch certain types of movies or listen to that kind music, but when nobody is around watch those types of movies and on occasions sing along to that type of music. Truth is if you put your hope in any human being you will eventually be let down because we are all hypocrites, we can't maintain a perfect status. **So let's start being honest, let's start declaring to the world, 'We are not perfect, we are not good', because in admitting our broken humanity, through the cracks shines God's divinity**. A strictly inclusive church doesn't deny that people are hypocritical it takes the attention off man and puts it on Jesus. It makes sure everyone's hope is in Jesus, because he is the only person to ever walk the earth without hypocrisy. We can put our hope in him for he will never let us down.

Let us pray and ask God to help us to always project to the world around us that there is plenty of room at the table. 'You can sit here; there is a place for you.' Let's take it even further and put our effort towards preparing a place for people, as if to say, 'We want you here. We have been waiting for you.'

CHAPTER SEVEN

The Rubix Cube

"You foolish Galatians! Who has bewitched you? Before your very eyes Jesus Christ was clearly portrayed as crucified. I would like to learn just one thing from you: Did you receive the Spirit by the works of the law, or by believing what you heard? Are you so foolish? After beginning by means of the Spirit, are you now trying to finish by means of the flesh? Have you experienced so much in vain—if it really was in vain? So again I ask, does God give you his Spirit and work miracles among you by the works of the law, or by your believing what you heard? So also Abraham "believed God, and it was credited to him as righteousness." Understand, then, that those who have faith are children of Abraham. Scripture foresaw that God would justify the Gentiles by faith, and announced the gospel in advance to Abraham: "All nations will be blessed through you." So those who rely on faith are blessed along with Abraham, the man of faith. For all who rely on the works of the law are under a curse, as it is written: "Cursed is everyone who does not continue to do everything written in the Book of the Law." Clearly no one who relies on the law is justified before God, because "the righteous will live by faith." The law is not based on faith; on the contrary, it says, "The person who does these things will live by them." Christ redeemed us from the curse of the law by becoming a curse for us, for it is written: "Cursed is everyone who is hung on a pole."[h] 14 He redeemed us in order that the blessing given to Abraham might come to the Gentiles through Christ Jesus, so that by faith we might receive the promise of the Spirit. (Galatians 3:1-14)

Years ago I was in northern California preaching for one of my friends. In between preaching we popped out to get a cup of 'glory' (a coffee) at the local mall. As we sat down to enjoy our delicious beverage I looked over and saw a guy at the table across from us and he was doing the most unusual thing. He reached into his pocket and pulled out a rubix cube, he then reached into his other pocket and pulled out a stopwatch. He then proceeded to open up his orange juice he had a sip, and put the lid back on. He pressed the stopwatch and quickly picked up the rubix cube and off he went, and a just a few seconds later, BAM, he pressed the stopwatch and the rubix cube was complete. All sides in there were matching colours. He quickly scrabbled the rubix cube into a multi colored mess had another sip of his orange juice, reset the stopwatch, pressed the start button and BAM off he went again. This time he completed the rubix cube even quicker. I was amazed to say the least. The only way I could ever complete a rubix cube was to take the colored stickers off and put them on the individual sides. If you ask me that is really the smart way to do it, none of this twisting business. Every time I tried a rubix cube I would manage to get one side matched up only to find all the other sides were out of whack. I think in the same way most of us have looked at the Christian life like a rubix cube. Just when you think you've got one thing nailed there is another area of your life still needing to be changed. It seems impossible. The reason why it seems impossible is because it is! If Christianity is about self-help, self-fixing, self-adjusting lifestyle, then we are all in trouble and the people around us are in trouble too. Why? Because you cannot keep up with that kind of change. If you can for a little while you will enforce it on others and lord it over them that you have changed and they have not.

When in honest fact you and I still have sides of our lives that don't match up, it seems like a never-ending process.

Here is my point. A strictly inclusive gospel is a simplistic gospel. It's not complicated. It is not a rubix cube and if it is, every which way you twist and turn it, all the sides will always match up to one thing. JESUS. He is the answer. In the time Jesus walked the earth mankind had tried to figure their way to God, they had created so many religious requirements and dogmas, so God came along in flesh, Jesus, and made it real simple by saying:

"Jesus answered, "I am the way and the truth and the life. No one comes to the Father except through me." (John 14:6)

My translation: "Guys, guys, guys, seriously stop it, you're making this too hard. I'm the way to do it, I'm the truth you need, and I'm the life you want."

A strictly inclusive church must be simplistic in its message.

So how do we preach a simplistic message? Well it's actually really simple.

Any message you preach, make Jesus the answer. Hold on? Isn't Jesus always the answer to every Christian message? Unfortunately not! Jesus is usually the answer to every altar call moment where people come to ask Jesus into their lives. But he is not always the point of the message. In the past I often found myself preaching messages that had a lot of potentially great life changing points, but not life giving Jesus focused points. The deference is a life changing point it is all about you going and trying to change your life with that point. A **life giving** point always leads to Jesus and he is the change agent who will ultimately bring change into our worlds.

Paul was adamant in keeping the gospel of Jesus Christ simple and attainable. The reason why he comes across seemingly harsh in this part of the Galatian letter is not necessarily because of the Galatians but because of the Judeazors. They didn't want the good news of the gospel to be strictly inclusive; they wanted it to be harder for people to get to God. They didn't want just any riffraff coming along and enjoying the goodness of God. They wanted an element of exclusivity. Not simplicity.

Here are some symptoms I believe of a church that leans towards exclusivity rather than simplicity:

1. So called Deep teaching rather than far reaching.

Ever heard people say, "I don't know about this church any more, I'm just not getting fed." I think this is the statement of a person who has lost sight of the simplicity of the gospel. Catch this, our maturity in Christ means we don't necessarily come to church on a Sunday to get fed (of course I think we can and do if our hearts are always open, and I believe every preacher's job is to equip the saints), but one of the greatest results of spiritual maturity is that I can now feed myself. I can indulge in the truths of the Bible every day. I don't rely only on the preacher to feed my soul on a Sunday. When we say I'm not getting fed, I'm saying I don't know how to feed myself.

Let's explore this 'Deep teaching' question further. What exactly is deep teaching? Does it mean I use deeper words or more Latin, Greek and Hebrew translations? Truth is the deeper I get the more simplistic it becomes. My understanding of deeper, is that the deeper I get the more I realize how insufficient I am and how amazingly sufficient God's grace is for me. We don't move on from the gospel, we go deeper into it. One of the most famous Scriptures in the Bible is John 3:16:

"For God so loved the world that he gave his one and only Son, that whoever believes in him shall not perish but have eternal life."

We have often written off this Scripture as elementary, when in fact it's not elementary it is foundational and simplistic. The more you know about Jesus the more simplistic his plans and purposes become, without a doubt the gospel has its mysteries, but one thing I know for sure is that God is passionately and unconditionally in love with humanity and it's our job to spread the message that our cities are 'so loved' by God. I'm all for **deeper study**, because I want to know Jesus more and what he has done for me, but the more I focus on Jesus, the more I love Jesus, and the more I find people loveable.

2. Legalistic rather than loving.

A major cause of church destruction and distraction is legalism. Legalism is demanding that people adhere to certain rules and requirements, and if they don't they can never have a relationship with God. Legalism is a strict way of living. Paul says to the Galatians: *"Are you so foolish? After beginning by means of the Spirit, are you now trying to finish by means of the flesh?"* In other words this didn't begin with your performance so why start making it performance driven now? The basic premise of legalism is man trying to qualify himself. Christ's death on the cross was our qualification, so if we continue to try and qualify ourselves by our performance then we are ultimately saying Jesus' death on the cross wasn't enough. The crazy and dangerous thing about legalism is that it is strangely comforting. It allows us to see and measure our own results. It is like a drug, when you're on it you feel on top of the world, the highest of highs, but when you come off it you experience the lowest of lows, it doesn't produce a sustainable state and it will leave you weak and wanting. A legalistic church forces people to live by self-performance rather than Christ's performance.

BUT before we go any further let's recognize that legalism is not to be confused with obedience to God. When God said' 'don't kill your neighbor,' you cannot say, 'well that's legalistic performance, I can do what I want.' NO, because of Christ's death on the cross you can obey God, you want to obey him, not because it earns you eternal brownie points, but because you LOVE HIM, you have a new nature.

In conclusion a legalistic church is not loving, it's demanding. As we love people and show them the goodness of God, people come to repentance (total trust) in God, not themselves. God's love is the most magnetic force to humanity. Legalism repels, but love compels people towards Jesus and his church.

3. Inward rather outward.

What we all long for is acceptance and belonging. We all check our instagram likes to see how many people thought we were awesome in that overly filtered selfie. When we find acceptance and belonging we are over the moon, we thrive off it to such a degree that we often forgot that there are others out there still searching to belong. We have all seen this happen in the church. Acceptance and belonging quickly turns into a cluster of small, tight knit people groups classically known as clicks. Often without intention they become extremely inward. As a church, 'clickiness' will be a non-stop constant battle. People will come to church and find their belonging, and their home, then enjoy the fact that they belong. The enjoyment often distracts us from the desire to want to include more people in this joy, because hey, I belong now and I've forgotten what it feels like not to belong.

Ever been to a church service and you've sat through it from start to finish and no one has ever welcomed or connected with you? It can often be an honest mistake, but most of the time it's because the comfort of 'clicks' has taken over and there is no room or no need to open up outward anymore. I love what Martin Luther said regarding an outward church:

> "THE CHURCH MUST RUN THE RISK OF DILUTION RATHER THAN LEAVE THE STATE TO THE COLD LIGHT OF REASON, UNWARMED BY TENDERNESS."

It's a risk to be inclusive, it's messy, it is uncomfortable. But it's a risk Christ was willing to take and so should we.

A strictly inclusive church is not about creating 'clicks', but doorways. Everywhere we go as friends in fellowship we don't go as 'clicks', but as warm welcoming doorways into fellowship and into the church. Imagine if everyone saw themselves as doorways with a big neon 'welcome' sign at the front? That is what an outward focused church looks like.

In summary a church that is simplistic is more attractive. Let's not forget Jesus was always trying to make God attainable where as the religious elite wanted to make a relationship with God unreachable.

Let's steer away from a complicated process and bring it back to its simplicity. Jesus died on the cross for people who didn't deserve it so that they could receive the life he deserved, a life with God, a life of abundance and eternal life. That's SIMPLY good news.

CHAPTER EIGHT

Gold Status

"For it is by grace you have been saved, through faith—and this is not from yourselves, it is the gift of God— not by works, so that no one can boast. (Ephesians 2:8-9)

I have had many great gifts given to me in my life, clothes, golf clubs, shoes, iPads (yeah I know right), and the gift of marriage! (thank the Lord I didn't receive the gift of celibacy, glory, glory, hallelujah!) But one the best gifts I have ever been given is a Gold status card to an international airline. A close friend of my mine who flies a lot called me up and told he had the ability to give me gold status just like him. I didn't need to do anything except give him my frequent flyer account number. Wwwhhhhhaaattttt. Little did I know the breadth of its benefits, seriously, no more waiting in lines to check in! You go straight to the first class check in and humbly wave at all the peasants as you walk by their crowded lines and down your red carpet to receive your ticket. It gets better! Instead of going to the wait in purgatory, I mean the airport terminal you go to the first class lounge. A magical place full of comfortable chairs, plasma TVs, your own barista who will meet your every caffeine needs, and wait for it… all you can eat food! The first class Gold status lounge often looks over on the terminal and as you look down you feel like royalty, and you know everyone else is looking back up at you with envy. I love the gold status. I love the VIP lounge and all its benefits.

One day I was sitting in the lounge enjoying all its benefits feeling pretty good about myself and quite frankly feeling more important than the other people in the entire airport terminal who didn't have the gold status, when suddenly I had a wake up call... "James. You didn't earn the gold status... you don't fly that much... you received it as a gift...You're really not better than anyone else down there in the terminal, the only reason you're sitting here is because of the kindness and generosity of someone else."

This to me is a perfect picture of grace and the good news of the gospel. We didn't earn it we received it as a gift, and not just a gift to keep to enjoy but a gift to be shared.

A strictly inclusive church doesn't just celebrate and receive the gift of grace, but distributes it!

One of the big things we have been journeying through as a church community is not so much methods but filters. We all want to bring about methods to create a church where people belong or methods of establishing people, or methods of making church awesome for those who are far from God and have never stepped into a church before. Don't get me wrong I'm all for methods, but I think it is better to start with filters. Why? **Methods will change as the world around us changes but our cultural church filters should stay the same.**

Our conclusion was that our filter for our church should be 'Strictly Inclusive'. It is through this filter that we pour all our methods.

Here are some great church methods that we found needed to go through our 'Strictly Inclusive' filter:

1. Our culture

The word culture comes from the word 'cultivate'. I don't know if you ever been in a green house or a glass house, but the idea behind it is that it is a structure or building that allows you to control the environment, what can grow or not grow. I love to think of our church as a green house where we can grow and nurture amazing life giving Christ centered environments. But what I've found is that we have actually made cultural environments that are massively exclusive rather than inclusive. We have taken Scriptures like 'Be in the world and not of it' and turned it into 'don't be in the world and have no culturally relevance what so ever.' ***We have made the church culture more about separation rather than 'infiltration'. We have made holiness about separation from the world around us and not about 'insulation' that happens on the inside of us by the Holy Spirit, that allows us to be an influence in our world.*** Jesus was always counter-cultural, or should I say he represented the real church culture. He went against the church's culture of his time, not because he wanted to be rebellious for rebellions sake, but he wanted to be culturally relevant for people's sake. There was a big difference between the Pharisees and Jesus. The Pharisees lived up to their name, the word Pharisee means 'separate' or 'the separated ones' to them being holy was to be separate from the world, but the word Holy means 'devoted, or devoted to God'. The Pharisees wanted to be separate from the world, where Jesus was devoted to God's plan for the world. Being in it to win it! Because of this we are going to have to kill some sacred cows.

I had an interesting conversation with a guy at church a while ago. He came up to me in a huff asking why are we playing 'Kanye West' in the pre-event church time, and my response was, why not? I like Kanye! (mind you we were not playing a track about booty shaking or dropping f-bombs) he couldn't believe it! He told me that when he became a Christian he burned all his 'worldly' music CDs, because it wasn't Christian. "Okay," I said, "its up to you what you want to do with your CD collection, and if you felt like it was best for you and your journey with God to do that, go for it, but the reason why we play this type of music before church is because we want to create a moment of cultural connection with any new people coming in. Church is already strange enough as it is, this is just a little minor way in which to destroy the myth that church has no understanding or cultural relevance to world around us. He was not happy with the response, but I continued, "Let me ask you this, do you still listen to the radio in the car? Or do you only listen to Christian music 24/7?"

"Umm well yeah," he responded.

"So how is that any different?" I said.

"Well the church is a holy place, for only holy things," he said.

"Yes I believe the church is holy because God is holy, but holiness is not a style of church, holiness is a state of the heart. Our intention in playing this music is not a compromise but a point of cultural connection to reach those far from God." I know as you are reading this your mind is struggling to digest that statement, something inside of you got all upset because you don't agree. But let me ask you this, why are you upset? Is it because God doesn't like unholy things? Or unholy cultures? God doesn't use worldly things to reach the world? OOOHHH I can not stop I have to go there. (big breath) Lets look at some of the ways God used cultural relevance as a vehicle to reach and relate to those far from him:

- **He used Daniel** in a Babylonian culture, he was head, the boss, the big cheese over all of the witches and the warlocks, he even dressed like them, he became so excellent in that culture (without compromising his beliefs) to the degree that the king was so impacted that he made everyone else worship Daniel's God (our God).

- **He used Joseph** in an Egyptian culture, he worked his way up the political ladder to become second in charge of all of Egypt. He didn't go against the culture he used it!

- **He used Esther** in a Persian culture to win the favor of King Xerxes (ok if you've seen 300 you know this guy was a bad mamajama and the Persian culture was crazy!) but she used her wisdom (and yes her good looks) to save her Jewish people all while living and using the culture around her.

- **He used Paul** in a Roman culture to influence an entire region! Paul would even quote the intellectual minds of their culture to use as a vehicle to win those who were far from God and to preach the gospel of Christ

I hope you're seeing my point, we should not run away from the culture we are trying to win, nor should we avoid using the culture around us as a means to win people to Christ. ***The point is - not people pleasing, but people winning***.

Look at what Christ prayed over his disciples:

*"**My prayer is not that you take them out of the world, but that you protect them from the evil one.**"* (John 17:15)

Jesus never wanted us to retreat from the culture and society around us, but be in it to win it! Not compromise our devotion to God but to comprise our separation from the world and sometimes compromise our methods in winning those people to Christ.

A strictly inclusive church uses and builds a culture that allows people beyond the walls of the church to feel included.

2. Our language

Based on my last point some of you have already concluded that what I mean by language is that we should be using more profanity to be relevant and dropping more f-bombs so that we are speaking the language of the world around us. Sorry to disappoint but that's not the language I'm talking about (I'm saving that for another chapter... just joking,). I have grown up in church almost my entire life and what I realized is we speak another language! Seriously. For example - we say things in conversation like in church:

"Greetings and salutations brethren aren't you glad you're washed in the blood

of the lamb and highly favored of the Lord Almighty."

Or

"I feel like the favor of God is going to flow like the rivers of Babylon into your life today."

Or

"I'm just so glad I live in desperation for the revelation of the divine tri-un God of all the ages, for ever and ever amen."

Ha! I know these are extremes, and it doesn't often happen like that, but what I've found is that a lot of what we say in church makes no sense to people who are not Christian. We use words that only make sense to people who have been around church for a long period of time, and when new people come in they feel excluded because quite frankly they don't get it.

What I love about Jesus is that he recognized that the people around him didn't understand God; they where confused on how to get to him, relate or communicate with him. The book of John says (my paraphrase) , "..He came to make the father known..." Why? People wanted to know God but they didn't know how to, and in their journey to know him they where becoming spiritually exhausted and bullied by religious leaders because they didn't know any difference. Jesus comes along and clearly, tangibly and powerful declares the simplicity of the good news of the gospel. While all the religious leaders loved the power of their knowledge, Jesus served up simple child like stories that made people of all walks of life come to hear him by the camel load (haha it was the Middle East could be foot or boat as well).

Check out what happens in Luke 15:1

"Now the tax collectors and 'sinners' were all gathering around to hear him."

As you read on you hear Jesus starting to tell three simple

stories that ultimately sum up the love God has for humanity. Jesus' language was engaging not just to temple (church) goers, but especially those who were far from God. Why? Because he wanted them especially to know that they were included in the church and the good news of the gospel.

As I type this I can hear some people thinking, 'James it seems like your methods are more about comprising the church to suit the world around us, are you trying to create a 'seeker sensitive' church?' Let me make something extremely clear, ***everything we do is NOT about watering down the gospel but simplifying it, which was always the way it was meant to be received***. There is nothing more attractive to a world full of brokenness and hopelessness than the simplicity of the gospel (I'll talk more about this in another chapter).

I'll finish with a challenging point and question:

"If we aren't attracting the same kind of people Jesus attracted, then maybe we aren't preaching the same message Jesus preached."

And here is my big question:

When you pour the 'language' of your church through the filter of strictly inclusive, does it leave those far from God engaged or excluded?

3. Our response

WARNING: Before we go any further I have to warn my readers by saying the subject I am going to touch on is rather sensitive, but I think I'm saying what most people are feeling and thinking.

Every Sunday at C3 Cronulla an amazing group of servant volunteers set up and pack up seats and so forth, for our church services. (I might be biased but we have the best team in the world!

Hands down). I was out the front with one of our team members pulling up the C3 Cronulla banner, when two women came out of the function hall we hire after attending another event, one of them stopped and asked what we where setting up. "A church actually," I responded. She looked down onto the banner to see big bold block letters saying 'STRICTLY INCLUSIVE', to which she replied, "Strictly inclusive huh?" in a slightly sarcastic tone. "How inclusive are you? Like same sex couples inclusive?" I could tell that as she said it she was expecting me to stutter and stammer my way through my response. "ABSOLUTELY," I responded without hesitation. You should have seen the look on her face; it was a beautiful mixture of shock, amazement and awe. "Oh, ok, maybe we will come sometime." As they walked away I could tell that response would stick with them for a long time. Let's talk about the elephant in the room shall we. Can you and I respond to a same sex couple with a confident response in your church? Remember it's not a matter of whether the church is pro-homosexual, the church is pro-homo sapiens. We don't have to agree with people to love people. We love people the same way Jesus loves people… unconditionally.

Our response to the world around us is not to agree with it, but to love it. The Bible is our truth, we don't have an opinion, but just because we don't agree with people and their lifestyles doesn't mean we can't love them and doesn't mean they cannot come to church. Where else will people hear the gospel? Where else will they find an atmosphere so charged with the Holy Spirit? Do we trust God enough to do the convicting and the changing?

I love this quote from Billy Graham.

> "IT'S GOD'S JOB TO JUDGE, THE HOLY SPIRIT'S
> JOB TO CONVICT AND OUR JOB TO LOVE."

A strictly inclusive church aims to respond the way Jesus wanted us to respond, with relentless Love. If you believe in the Holy

Spirit don't try to be him… trust him.

Remember you don't have to agree with people to love people.
By the grace of God we ALL (every single person on the planet) have been given the opportunity to part take in the VIP Gold status of God's grace through Jesus and once we've got it, to remember that we didn't earn it and we are not just allowed to share it, we are commissioned to share it.

Gold Status

CHAPTER NINE

The Obituary of A Ministry

"To the church of the Thessalonians in God the Father and the Lord Jesus Christ:

Grace and peace to you. We always thank God for all of you and continually mention you in our prayers. We remember before our God and Father your work produced by faith, your labor prompted by love, and your endurance inspired by hope in our Lord Jesus Christ." 1 Thessalonians 1:1-3

I have a confession to make... I am a massive documentary fan! I love them. I like just about every kind of documentary, except the ones about the 'Great Depression'... too depressing. The documentaries that I really love are the animal documentaries, and I don't mean the ones about the sleeping pattern of south east Asian sloth (but I have seen it). I mean the documentaries like, 'When animals attack' or 'The world's most deadliest' or 'Big Cats'. Seriously how carnal are we in those leopard documentaries? One second we are cheering on the leopard as he chases down the baby gazelle, "Get him! Take him down," then as soon as he comes close our hearts are breaking for the baby gazelle "Come on little fella, you can do it, run like the wind, you're going to make it, you've got a future." Then when the leopard finally gets him we have mixed emotions, "Yeah he got him!" Then a second later, "That's so sad, I hate leopards, why didn't the camera man do something."

The documentary that tops them all off are the shark documentaries

(I can hear you right now responding as you read this with a YEAH). Mind you, this doesn't help when you've grown up on the beach. My imagination is good enough without the help of great white shark documentary images flashing through my head as you are about to duck dive under a wave. Or when you are sitting out the back of the surf at dusk. I always picture myself in a *Jaws* scene where I am being thrown back and forth in the surf yelling, "that's not snow flake!" (Sorry that's for all the *Ace Ventura* fans out there.)

The point for my rambling was something that really made me think one day as I was watching a shark documentary. A sad story was being told of a young north Californian surfer who lost his life in a shark attack. The documentary showed interviews with the young man's family and friends talking about how much they would miss their friend. One of the repeated comments that struck me the most was the statement of how he will be remembered. A familiar statement we've all heard before, "He died doing what he loved." My thought instantly was how would I be remembered? What will they say about me? This then caused me to approach it from a whole different angle.

"How will our church be remembered?"

"What will they say about us?"

I am in no way predicting a premature death of our church or any church, but sometimes it is better to work backwards from the end result. So I started to write down what I hoped to be the obituary of our ministry or our church. This is what I believe Jesus would want to have written about his church:

1. It wasn't about how cool our ministry looked, but how people felt like they belonged when they walked in.

I love church that is excellent in every way. I believe that everything we do should give glory to God, but I have found myself sometimes focusing more on how cool my ministry looked as opposed to focusing on the people it is intended to reach. Here's the thing, in all my years of doing ministry I have never once seen someone come to the front to respond to Christ and as I approached them and asked them why they are making this decision they looked up at me through tear filled eyes and burst out "it was the LED screen, I just saw it flashing cool images and graphics and I just felt so convicted of my sins that I ran to the altar!" I never heard this response, but what I have heard most of the times was, "My friend has been inviting me for along time and I just felt like I belonged here and I wanted to know more about Jesus."

Please don't get me wrong I believe we should always be relevant in our methods of church, but what I found to be true is that cool church more often attracts more Christians, REAL church attracts people who are far from God. A real inclusive relationship far out ways a really big production system.

2. It wasn't about perfect people, but about people who persistently pursued Jesus and people.

When people think of church they think of good people. Or that's the place where good people gather. I wonder when this idea changed? Based on the message of Christ it wasn't the healthy who needed a doctor, but the sick, so really the church isn't a gathering of good people at all, it's a gathering of soul sick, sinful people. The idea that you need to prefabricate and perfect yourself before you come to church, is like a sick person trying to get healthy before they went to the hospital?? It doesn't make sense. We need to re-brand the church to the world around us; if you have issues the church is the place you go. God can only work with messed up people, because messed up people are all that there are. The church isn't a museum of saints but a hospital for sinners. Our aim should be to journey with one another as we continue to encourage each other towards Christ. The journey is not a perfect one, but it is a persistent one. I hope we are remembered for our commitment to journey with people towards Jesus, through thick or thin, ups and downs, goods times and especially bad times.

3. It wasn't about how much they could prove the point that humanity is wrong, but to show humanity how much it is loved by Jesus.

The church is often known for what it is against, and rarely known for what it is for. It breaks my heart to see Christians waving their picket signs with bold words written on them about God's hate and anger towards them. I have never known or even heard of anyone coming to God because they saw a sign that said God hates them and thought, 'Wow I don't want that, I had better change and follow God.' It just doesn't happen. The Bible is clear:

"Or do you show contempt for the riches of his kindness, forbearance and patience, not realizing that God's kindness is intended to lead you to repentance?" – Romans 2:4 (NIV)

The point of the Christian or the church is not to go around trying to prove that people are wrong, our mission is to show the kindness of God. I hope we are remembered for our consistency to show the love and kindness of Christ to the world around us.

4. It wasn't a place where people threw stones of judgment, but rolled away stones that are keeping people from getting to Jesus.

I realize this point seems reasonably similar to the last, but I felt it required its own little section. What I've found to be true in my own life is that I often throw stones of judgment at the things or people I don't understand. It is so easy to judge the book by its cover. The woman caught in the act of adultery in John 8 is the perfect example of a stone-throwing situation. All the crowd around her knew the head lines of what she had done, but neglected to try and know the details. The truth is the women wasn't innocent, she was caught in the act of her sin, but I wonder if our response would change towards her if we knew her past? The Bible doesn't tell us anything about it, but maybe she grew up in a household with a father or a relative who sexually abused her? Or maybe she grew up in a household where the father was absent and in her pursuit of affirmation from a man she found herself in situations where men took advantage or her? Or maybe she grew up on the streets and the only way she could survive was to attach herself to men who would in-turn give her shelter or money. All this is speculation, but as you are reading this I am sure your heart towards her is not growing callas with distain, but softer with compassion. *I think we would easily change our response to broken people, if we took time to find out what broke them.*

A strictly inclusive church seeks to know the broken person, not judge their brokenness.

5. **It wasn't about how well known we became but how famous we made Jesus.**

Sometimes in our pursuit of becoming a cool relevant church we can easily get side tracked trying to make our churches more famous rather than making Jesus famous. So often I have walked away from a church service worrying about the wrong things, the music was too loud, the music was too soft, people didn't laugh or engage enough in my message, the screens didn't work properly, and so forth. Check out what Colossians says:

"And whatever you do, in word or deed, do everything in the name of the Lord Jesus, giving thanks to God the Father through him." Colossians 3:17 (ESV)

Without a doubt this scripture is promoting the fact that we should do everything well, but the aim of excellence isn't the fame of a church brand or just any person, we are to do it for the glory of Jesus. I think the success of a Sunday would be tested by how much more people think and talk about Jesus.

A strictly inclusive church's aim is to see the name of Jesus made famous!

6. It wasn't about who served them, but who they can serve?

Many years ago I heard a story of a reporter who wanted to investigate the source of happiness. What causes it or how to achieve true happiness? So he started by interviewing someone of notable wealth and fame, he went to interview the pop icon Madonna. As he arrived at her opulent property and drove up to her mansion he was greeted by one of the staff there and was led up to the room where Madonna could give her interview, the house was amazing to say the least. The room where the interview was to be held was filled with platinum records and music awards, and as the reporter sat down he quickly got straight to the point. "Madonna your house is amazing and it is obvious that money and fame is not an issue for you, you must be one happy lady?" To his shock Madonna responded, "Actually no, I'm not happy and I don't know anyone who is truly happy."

The reporter had another person he also wanted to interview, who was famous but for different reasons. He began his journey to see his next interviewee, except she wasn't in a wealthy property surrounded by fame and fortune, she was in the slums of a place called Calcutta in India, her name was Anjeze Gonxhe Bojaxhiu otherwise known as Mother Teresa. When he arrived she was not at her living quarters and he was told she was out where she usually was, in the streets of the poorest neighborhoods in Calcutta. He found her in the streets tending to a man who was suffering from leprosy. His flesh rotted and his wounds filled with infection, but there she was holding him tending to his wounds. The reporter introduced himself with a tissue covering his nose and commented, "Mother Teresa I would not do what you're doing for a million dollars!" To which she replied with a smile on her face, "Neither would I," and she continued to wipe his wounds. What amazed the reporter the most was the fact that Mother Teresa was so full of happiness and joy.

We live in a world that is seeking to BE served, for when WE are served it shows that we are of more importance. The more we have and the more people who can serve us the happier we will be. But truth is the antithesis of that. The more we serve others the happier we become. Christ served us through the cross and gave to us everything we will ever need. Now we are free to serve others without any agenda. AMAZING! What great freedom we find when we no longer look to others to serve our egos, but are secure enough in Christ to serve others.

I think it's not just the way we behave that will inspire people towards Christ, but the way that we serve that leads people to Christ.

A strictly inclusive church is a church secure enough to serve. Regardless of whether we will get anything in return.

7. It wasn't about clicks it was about door ways.

A great movie came out a few years ago called *The Village*. The basic plot is about a group of broken and scared people who decide to build their own little village so they would be safe from the corruption of the outside world. Nobody comes in and nobody goes out. While I really enjoyed the movie, it breaks my heart to find that a lot of churches operate the same way. Holy huddles or Christian 'clicks' are unfortunately too common in the world today. The amount of stories I have heard about people going into churches and never being welcomed, or greeted or engaged with are too many to number. We must recognize that 'clicks' are a natural part of life, once we find comfort we don't like to disrupt it and new people might just do that. A strictly inclusive church is the opposite of a clicky church. We are a church of reconciliation.

19th Century theologian Karl Niebuhr said it like this:

> "RECONCILIATION MEANS TURNING TO GOD, A
> LOYALTY TO GOD AND TO THE THINGS OF GOD,
> "PATRIOTISM OF THE UNIVERSAL COMMONWEALTH"
> DISPLACING CONSTRICTED LOVES TO CLOSED SOCIETIES

THAT RENDER US DISLOYAL TO THOSE BEYOND
THEIR BORDERS AND BOUNDARIES. RECONCILIATION
MEANS BEING CAUGHT IN THE GRIPS OF AN
EXPANSIVE LOVE OF GOD AND NEIGHBOUR…"

Man I love that statement. We put aside constricted love that 'clicks' produce. We can't help but share the expansive love of God to the world around us. You see, yours and my life is a doorway with a huge flashing neon sign at the top declaring that you are welcome, come and be a part of the community of Christ.

A strictly inclusive church rages against 'clicks' and strives to create doorways that others go through to get closer to Christ.

8. They took risks on people and believed in them.

There is nothing more risky than Grace. Grace overlooks the fact that David was just a teenage shepherd boy with no experience in 'giant killing' and stirs him to step up and go for it. Grace embraces a crooked tax collector called Levi (Matthew) and asks him to join the greatest mission the world had ever seen. Grace confronts a religious Christian arresting fanatic called Saul (Paul) and uses him to deliver the gospel to an entire region of the world…I don't know about you but GRACE IS RISKY!! Truth is none of us would be doing what we are doing unless someone took a risk on us and believed in us. Mind you grace doesn't overlook faults and failings, it brings them into light and transforms them into a God glorifying masterpiece. Nobody comes prefabricated and perfect it all starts with taking a risk. In following the example of Jesus who welcomed the worst but believed the best, a strictly inclusive church is one that is known for taking risks on people and believing in them even when others don't.

My hope is that when it comes to the end of our time in ministry I pray that these things will be said about our churches. I truly believe that a Christ centered church reflects all these things and more. If there ever were such a thing as an obituary of a ministry all these qualities should be evident in all our churches.

CHAPTER TEN

Furious Love

Here is a trustworthy saying that deserves full acceptance: *"Christ Jesus came into the world to save sinners—of whom I am the worst. 16 But for that very reason I was shown mercy so that in me, the worst of sinners, Christ Jesus might display his immense patience as an example for those who would believe in him and receive eternal life."* 1 Timothy 1:15-16

I have to be honest I'm not a book person (funny because I'm writing one!! Go figure) I am more of a movie person. That's right when it came to reading books at school I prayed that they had also made it into a movie, that way I could simply sit down on the lounge and save hours of my life through the pressing of a button. I find it so funny when they make a book into a movie and all the book readers throw their hands up in disgust faulting the movie because they clearly missed intricate details from the book. Whereas I will never have that problem because I will never know any better, and to be honest I think it makes it more enjoyable with the help of a fridge box sized popcorn and a bath sized coke! Ha!

One of the greatest films I've seen is a movie called *Fury*. If you seen it you just let out and audible "YESSSSSSSS" to which people around you stopped and stared. It is a classic romantic comedy, just joking! It's just straight up blood, guts and violence. In the movie, four men man a tank during World War 2 captained by Captain Don 'Wardaddy' Collier (Brad Pitt). One of the other main characters in the movie is Boyd 'Bible' Swan, played by Shia LaBeouf. Boyd is a Christian man who throughout the entire film quotes Scripture, leads people to Jesus as they lay dying, and so on. What's amazing is that the fictional character had quite an effect on Shia Labeouf who after the film made a public statement that he gave his life to God, but what really got me interested was the statement Shia made about his newfound relationship with God:

> "I BECAME A CHRISTIAN MAN AND NOT IN A @#$
> #%^*%! WAY, BUT IN A VERY REAL WAY."

Don't you just love this! You see what most people focused on was the colorful language that played a part in this statement and totally overlooked the bold declaration that over shadowed every other part; he is now a Christian man!

What broke my heart was the Christian bloggers who quickly pounced onto his confession and immediately shut it down, because if he is a Christian man then he wouldn't have sworn like that..... WWWWHAAATTTT... wait a second, can we really write off the validity of his salvation merely because he used profanity?

Let's look at one of the key figures in the early church, the first pastor, pope or leader, our good friend Peter. Peter was a man who walked with Jesus in the flesh for the entire three years of his earthly ministry, he ate with him, ministered with him, prayed with him, but even with all that time with Jesus Peter still had a language problem and an anger issue, to the point where just before Jesus crucifixion he did two pretty outrageous things, he cut off a guy's ear and swore at a teenage girl! (Talk about issues) But how did Jesus react? Jesus loved him, and with immense patience he persistently pursued Peter even when his performance or behavior was well below par.

Why? God's furious love!

God's furious love is not restricted by our performance, but is characteristically relentless due to his unlimited patience.

In order to be a strictly inclusive church we need to understand that transformation doesn't occur in a person's life due to man made performance checks. But through unlimited patience, trusting in God's furious love, and the power of the Holy spirit. Salvation is a moment, but transformation is a journey.

We pray crazy prayers like "God let your church be filled" and then God starts filling his church. It's at this point we quickly realize that people don't come pre-fabricated and perfect, but they come in swearing, broken, bruised, and RAW! This is where Paul's trustworthy statement comes into full effect.

Paul reveals two epic truths about the nature of God and what should be reflected in the nature of the church:

1. God came to pursue sinners, even the worst.

Before we disqualify someone or ourselves due to our behavior, reflect upon Paul. The self titled worst of sinners. He didn't just say some bad words, or look at something bad on the Internet, he was in charge of killing Christians!! He was truly the best at being the worst, but God pursued him. Sometimes we write off the ones that God's grace is extended towards because we forget that his furious love came to consume sinners, even the worst. It wasn't the behavior of humanity that attracted God to send his one and only Son, but his furious Love.

When grace put on flesh and walked this earth two thousand odd years ago, Jesus was always hanging out with people who society labeled the worst, the religious leaders of his time muttered about his actions questioning why he would do that, Jesus response was, "It's not the healthy who need a doctor but the sick." What we can easily lose sight of is the point Jesus was making. There are no healthy people! We are all sick in soul because of sin and He, the master physician, came to bring the only cure that can work, salvation through the forgiveness and grace of God!

The message of a strictly inclusive church isn't 'get yourself better before God can accept you', but come the way you are and let the grace of God heal and change you.

2. God has unlimited patience.

I am so glad that God's patience has no shelf life it does not unexpectantly expire on me. It is unlimited, even though we keep dropping the ball he keeps giving us another chance. Because of this unlimited patience his grace ultimately has its way in my life. As much as we try to fight against it, its relentless persistency overpowers us and we find ourselves giving up to the furious love of God. It is this same furious love that like Paul the apostle says 'compels us' to never give up on people but to keep displaying patience through consistent love.

Patience has a massive part to play in the reaching and raising disciples for Jesus.

I don't know about you but patience isn't always my strong point, so how can I be expected to display unlimited patience? Treat every person the same way God treats us, like his children.

Years ago I had a pastoral situation I had to attend to, a member of our church was making some huge mistakes that had to be addressed. I had already sat down with this person multiple times about the same issue and now it had happened again. I was mad! I was driving to meet him and my mind was set on asking him to leave the church. As I started to pray to ask for peace and not anger, I felt God say to me, 'Treat him like you would treat your son Bailey. What? Excuse me? Come again? "Treat him like you would treat your son Bailey." Suddenly it was like God's furious love struck my heart. If I truly treated this person like my son, then yes I would disciple him, and I would do whatever it took to make sure he knew I loved him. That he was staying in church and that I was not going to give up on him. I can you tell the meeting was strong, but the presence of God's love was thick. To this day not only is that person still in church but he loves Christ and is happily married.

My patience in this situation was fueled by love and if love is the fuel, patience is never running out.

God's furious love leads people to the point of salvation and beyond, but what I've found to be true is that salvation is a moment, and transformation is a journey. Let us follow in the likeness of God and pursue people and tell them about God's furious relentless love for them and love them through the journey of transformation.

I hope that our churches are full of swearing new followers of Christ rather than mostly empty rooms filled with performance driven, judgment focused people who have lost sight of a trustworthy saying that Christ Jesus came into the world to save the worst of sinners. Jesus welcomed the worst and believed the best!

So here's the questions I have to ask myself and we must ask ourselves about our lives and our churches.

- *Does my life, and my church, demonstrate God's furious love?*

- *Does it demonstrate God's 'intentional' pursuit of all people, even the worst?*

- *Are we displaying God's unlimited patience towards the people God brings into our churches and our world?*

- *Are we willing to commit to the journey with people, even when patience is wearing thin?*

CHAPTER ELEVEN

The Danger of Inclusion

I love old historical churches. I love the architecture and the grandeur of their design. I love the fact that in the process of someone conceiving its construction, that person must have been thinking, 'I want to design a building that brings glory to God, a beautiful reflection of the magnificence and breath taking awesomeness of God', and from that place they wanted to somehow show that to the world through the design. Interesting to note that when these beautiful churches where built they weren't just built for the existing members of the church, they where built to inspire and compel other people to come and see and hear about the good news of the gospel. So much so that you will notice on the stain glass windows of these old cathedrals, even today, you'll see that pictures depicting Jesus and different gospel stories on the windows and they are facing *outwards.* The picture message of our loving shepherd, savior and king are being displayed to tell a message to those outside the church building, not just inside, this my friends is the very heart beat of a strictly inclusive church!!

I truly believe deep down inside that we are all trying to create strictly inclusive churches, but how do we let this culture and truth transcend our theory to make it an intentional practice.

Study shows that social exclusion heightens people's desire to forge new relationships. Seems pretty obvious - when we feel left out we go looking for new relationships. Thing is the opposite is also true. When people feel INCLUDED the drive to create new relationships is reduced. This has pretty solid implications for evangelism and people reaching out. Ironically, when people feel included they are less likely to include others. So how do we keep a strictly inclusive community? We build an authentic community.

I don't know if you have ever been to Bali or Thailand or a part of the world that is know for it cheap imitation products. I remember going to Thailand with my wife and buying her an imitation Prada bag. It looked exactly the same as the original, to the untrained eye you would never know any different, and even better it was one hundredth of the price (I am not cheap...just wise...kind of). The issue was that it was only six months after the purchase that the seams started to split and the bag started to fall apart. I found out quickly that imitation substitutes one very important thing....quality! So why do people buy imitation products? Because we want the product but aren't willing to pay the price, but if we pay the price and we get the authentic real deal, it lasts the distance.

In Acts 2 we start to see the original church and the perfect demonstration of a real deal authentic community. What we must take note of straight away is that they all did something quite remarkable. Verse 24 says they *devoted themselves*. No one told them to, they didn't need to constantly be encouraged or pushed, they made a decision to devote themselves. It was a personal decision. They calculated the cost and were willing to pay it.

What they devoted themselves to was what I believe made them an authentic community:

1. They devote themselves to the teachings of Jesus.

The fountain of authentic community comes from Christ himself. When we read the writing of Matthew, Mark, Luke and John we see the consistent character of Jesus and his willingness to include others and lead others to do the same. Truly Jesus was inclusive and the more we study about his inclusive love for us and others through the work of the cross we can't help but respond by loving him and loving others. When I was a little boy I had a fascination with staring at the sun, you know...the big ball of fire in the sky. My mum would always tell me, "James stop staring at the sun, you will burn your retina!" But while she wasn't looking I went back to staring. When you took your eyes off the sun, all you could see was a black sun shaped silhouette on everything you looked at. I believe in the same way the more we devote ourselves to focusing on the SON of God, Jesus, the more we will see his silhouette on everyone we encounter.

2. They devoted themselves to fellowship.

Fellowship isn't always convenient, it takes devotion and commitment. We by nature prefer to take the path of least resistance. Fellowship means me taking my time and investing it into others, even sometimes when I don't feel like it. On the other side fellowship is good for us. We need fellow believers around us. When I was on a flight recently they handed out hot towels to cleanse your face and make you feel comfortable before you took off. As I peered down the isle from row one thousand and twenty I noticed that the tray of towels was steaming hot, to the point where the air hostess was using tongs to hand them out to prevent burning her hand. I thought sure by the time she got to me the towels would have cooled down. But when I received my towel it was still steaming hot, literally 10 seconds after I had handled the lone towel it had already cooled down. I quickly realized that towels alone couldn't remain hot, but together they could. In the same way the fire and heat of our faith is kept constant by the consistent togetherness of the saints. We are better together. The book of Acts' church was so together and devoted to fellowship it's no wonder they had such fervent faith.

3. We devotes ourselves to sharing life together (eating together).

In an ancient Middle Eastern time to eat with someone wasn't a shallow food based occasion, it was considered an invitation to do life with someone. To invite someone to dinner was to invite them to share your life. The equivalent today would be like someone inviting you over to their house and after eating a meeting together they handed you a key to their house and said, "Me casa su casa" - in other words, what's mine is yours. Crazy right! That is exactly what the books of Acts community did. Now let's get serious, should we hand out keys to our house to any person who joins our church community? NO! But we should reflect upon how we open our lives to others. Do I compartmentalize my Christian community moments to just one and half hours on a Sunday? If we are truly to attain that sense and reality of a strictly inclusive community we must be willing to share our lives. To share meals with each other, to let our hair down and laugh and cry, eat and drink together through sharing of meals in our homes. Our aim is not to include people into a church crowd, but introduce them into a loving and sharing church community.

4. We devote ourselves to prayer

When I first left high school I wasn't too sure what I wanted to do with my life so I decided to become a carpenter (like Jesus). At one point as an apprentice I was asked to be the laborer for our bricky (builders' talk for brick layer). My awesome exciting task was to move a pallet full of bricks from the front of the house block to the back where the brick layer was building the walls to make the house. During the task I started to think what separates the pile of bricks from the front of the block to the pile of bricks at the back of the yard? I mean it's the same bricks and they are still going into a pile? The simple difference, one pile of bricks are piled together, the other are glued together. One pile all though still heavy and strong with just a little bit of force, could come tumbling down, the ones that are glued together take a lot to separate them. In a similar way each one of us are the bricks that make up the house of God and what will separate us from the pile people that comprise any other community, is the foundation that we are built on which is Jesus. The glue that holds us together, which is our prayer for one another. When we take time to pray for one another we strengthen community. Prayer for others gives me compassion for others, prayer for others gives love for others, and prayer for others gives me patience for others. Have you ever noticed it is really hard to not like a person when you pray for them? Why? Prayer is you decreasing and the Holy Spirit increasing in our lives, his nature counteracting ours. A strictly inclusive community doesn't just pray for the world around us, it prays for each other.

5. We devote ourselves to generosity.

When you get invited to a person's birthday party who you barely know, you don't usually go out of your way to buy them an expensive gift, but when it's your wife, your husband or someone extremely close, price is not an issue. If anything the expense can determine the depth of the relationship. Generosity is birthed out of affection. You give to what you love. On the other hand ironically what we give to also causes our affections to grow fonder. Where your treasure is your heart will be also. When we give to one another we fuel the fire of intimate community. Our mind is tricked into loving that person more. Know this, generosity isn't a response to obligation; it's a response to freedom. Free people give freely. An authentic community is a group of people who have experienced the love and freedom of Christ and now money and possessions are no longer things that rule our lives. Generosity is a reaction to the generous love and freedom we have received from God through Jesus.

6. We devote ourselves to worshipping Jesus

I was once invited to preach in the beautiful country of Denmark. It's quite amazing going to countries that are far older than your own. So much rich history and culture! On a side note I have to mention that everyone there is six foot four, with perfect blonde hair with an athletic build, I obviously felt comfortable there (minus a few qualities.) We arrived at the conference I was to speak at. The place was full of excitement and anticipation. The worship began and the sound of Danish saints in worship began to rise, I couldn't understand a word they where singing but I couldn't help but worship. Why? Worship is universal. You could be in a room full of every culture and ethnicity in the world but united in worship because the centerpiece of the worship is the same person. JESUS. What I found to be true is that worship unites us. It's like going to a sports game of your favorite team, with fans from all over, and when your team wins and you start chanting the name of your team. Even the strangers in the crowd around you become your best friend because they support the same team. As followers of Christ we are all united in his team, the winning team, and worship is our celebratory song that brings us together.

All these qualities were the foundation of the early church and I believe as we strive to keep them we will continue to see an authentic community grow. Understand it is something we must fight for, it will not happen by osmosis, it takes intentionality and strength to fight to keep our communities inclusive. It is a worthwhile fight that we must make every day in our own lives to fight against the comfort of exclusion and fight with our own preferences and feelings towards others so that they too might be included in the glorious love of God.

CHAPTER TWELVE

Eliminating the Steps Between Us

(THE STRUGGLE OF INCLUSION)

"But when Cephas came to Antioch, I opposed him to his face, because he stood condemned. For before certain men came from James, he was eating with the Gentiles; but when they came he drew back and separated himself, fearing the circumcision party. And the rest of the Jews acted hypocritically along with him, so that even Barnabas was led astray by their hypocrisy. But when I saw that their conduct was not in step with the truth of the gospel, I said to Cephas before them all, "If you, though a Jew, live like a Gentile and not like a Jew, how can you force the Gentiles to live like Jews?" Galatians 2:11-13

A s I mentioned earlier in this book, I am a huge ancient history buff, especially Church history. Years ago I was lucky enough to do the ancient church tour in Rome. It was truly amazing visiting all the sites of the early church. But as much as it had its awe and wonder it also had some sad moments. One particular day we visited one of the old Catholic churches and joined in on a tour group. By joined in I mean we just pretended we were part of the group and got a free guided tour. During the tour of this particular church, the tour guide starting pointing out the church relics that had been housed behind thick platted glass. "Here is a splinter of the cross of Christ." Suddenly the tour group gasped and the camera flashes filled the air like New Years Eve fire works as they marveled as this tiny fracture of timber. "Here in this golden coffin are the heads of Peter and John the Baptist." Again the crowd couldn't help but be overwhelmed by this miraculous spectacle. And at that I couldn't help but put my hand in the air and call out, "Excuse me, excuse me, how do you know that the splinter was from the cross of Christ and the heads belonged to Paul and John?" The tour guide looked at me as if I had just asked him to explain the mind of a women, "ummm….Time to move on, so much more to see." The next part of the tour brought us to one of the most world renowned relics, 'Sancta Scalla' a staircase that is believed to be the very staircase that Jesus walked up to meet with Pontius Pilate to receive his death sentence. He then walked back down on the journey to the cross. People believe that if you get on your knees and pray on each step, the higher you go, the more your sins are forgiven and closer you get to God. What amazed me about this staircase was seeing multitudes of people filling each step, hoping and praying that through these actions God will react and grant them forgiveness and closeness. At that point I wanted to shout to them all the good news of the gospel. The good news that God didn't wait for us to climb each step to find forgiveness and closeness, NO! He met us on the bottom step to offer us the gift of his forgiveness and closeness by his grace through his son Jesus. Such amazingly life changing news! The message of a strictly inclusive church is that God meets all of us on the bottom step! If you don't know that, well I hope this helps. If this is true, which it is, then why will a strictly inclusive church still encounter problems with inclusion?

I heard a preacher say recently: *"A lot of people admit that we have all fallen short of the glory of God, but we still measure distances."*

It is amazing how much truth this statement holds - so much truth. We all know we need grace, but we have convinced ourselves that some need it more than others. We all know we have fallen short, but if we are honest with ourselves we are convinced that we fell a little closer to the glory than others did. As much as we look at literal 'Sancta Scala' and cannot believe people would do that, we have actually created our own staircase in our minds. We look at others and truth be told we either see them a few steps ahead of us, but mostly we see them a few steps behind us. We see the person with the addiction, the young man struggling with his sexuality, the girl who cuts herself and struggles with self-esteem, and the man with the broken marriage, as a few steps behind us. We don't verbalize it, but we think it. We have created our own 'Sancta Scala'. We count the steps between them and us.

In order to create an inclusive community we must understand the complexities and difficulties that lie ahead. As soon as you start preaching and declaring this message and creating a culture of inclusion there are going to be road bumps and hurdles that riddle the road ahead. You see just about everyone agrees with the strictly inclusive message. You have read this book over and over again and have found yourself vehemently agreeing with its principles. Yes we should be an inclusive community. Yes we should be a hospital of hope for humanity and not a country club for the morally elite. It's at this point that we must recognize that everyone agrees with the principles, but until their paradigm (their life and actions) reflects those principles, it doesn't matter. In other words the day we become a strictly inclusive community is the day when what we preach becomes what we live, act and do. So how do we lead our church communities through the difficult journey of truly becoming a strictly inclusive church?

It's at this point we must look to the early church. We read Acts 2 and we see this inclusive community of Jesus lovers eating together, opening up each other's homes and lives. Generously giving to one another without agenda. But let us remember that the first church mentioned in Acts 2 was predominately made up of Jews. They all fundamentally shared the same principles and paradigms, it was only when the church started to spread beyond Jerusalem that we start to encounter the struggles with inclusion. The gospel had spread like an unpredictable wild fire all the way to the Gentile city of Antioch. It's at this point the church started to feel the stress and strain of an inclusive church, because now the gospel had flung open the doors to welcome everyone, not just Jews or people who adhered to Jewish custom. The gospel was a welcome mat laid out for all to see with the intention that all would see they are welcomed into relationship with God through his son Jesus. You would think it would be easy to spread and share such incredible news. But the book of Galatians shows us that the reality of God's inclusive love and grace hadn't really hit home with Peter, Barnabas and those who came from James in Jerusalem. They agreed with the principle but their paradigm didn't match. This is something we also should expect. It will not be a walk in the park to create and foster a strictly inclusive community. So how do we navigate through these uncharted waters in our church communities? Galatians 2 shows us the four ways in which I believe we handle the struggle of inclusion:

1. Understanding how religious I still am.

What I fail to recognize in myself is how religious I still am. What do I mean by religious? I mean I am still given to live by my own performance and judge other people on theirs. There is still a little bit of Pharisee in me. I still am given to the default position of my flesh, which wants to judge others. Peter was a man who had rejected and denied Jesus three times, but instead of receiving the same response from Christ, he encountered complete forgiveness and inclusion from Jesus. He of all people, should be the poster child of love and inclusion, but even the great Apostle Peter found himself slipping into a religious exclusive mindset. What does this tell us? That we too can find ourselves in the same place, we are all susceptible to being exclusive especially when the people we are dealing with are not similar to us. I don't know if we will ever truly drown out the Pharisaical voice that often pops up in our minds, so the question is how do we overcome it? We must firstly admit that we are given to judging others. It will always be the opposing voice that tries to drown out the voice of grace. Secondly we should remember the piercing words that Jesus used to shut down the Pharisees when they threatened to stone the adulterous woman, *"Let he who is without sin, cast the first sin."* The only way to confront the Pharisee in me is to remind myself that I deserved the stones. I deserved to be rejected by God for my actions, but Jesus stepped in and received the stoning on my behalf through his work on the cross so that I could have relationship and forgiveness with God. Understanding my own religiosity and reminding myself of God's merciful response towards me gives me a sober understanding of myself. It reminds me how I should love and treat others. When the Pharisee in me rises I need to, at that point, remember that I must include or accept others as Christ has accepted me (Romans 15:7).

2. Recognize the discomfort of inclusion.

I would love to tell you that this inclusion thing will be easy and that your church community will be overjoyed to accept and include others, but this 'inclusion' thing is uncomfortable. As much as people will agree with the principle it will be challenging to actually live it out. Can you image the scene that took place in Galatians 2, every week the community of Christ would gather together for what was referred to as the 'agape feast' or the love feast? To eat together was more than just a meal, it was the sharing of each other's lives. To eat with someone was to declare to others 'I'm doing life with this person'. The 'agape feast' was an array of awkward diversity, rich would sit with poor, slaves would eat with free people, Jews would share drinks with Gentiles. We must understand that this radically flew in the face of the existing culture it was truly counter-cultural. But the question we must ask is: 'Was it easy for them to do this?' And the answer would undeniably be 'NO' it would have been full of tension and awkward social moments. So how did they do it? They chose to focus not on what divides them but on what united them. JESUS. He was the reason they could sit in such rich diversity. This topic of unity amongst diversity was a constant reminder that Paul often gave to the church:

"So if there is any encouragement in Christ, any comfort from love, any participation in the Spirit, any affection and sympathy, complete my joy by being of the same mind, having the same love, being in full accord and of one mind. Do nothing from selfish ambition or conceit, but in humility count others more significant than yourselves. Let each of you look not only to his own interests, but also to the interests of others. " (Philippians 2:1-4)

You see an inclusive community isn't created because everyone has everything in common and everyone has it together. It is created because everyone is willing to put up with each other's uncommon-ness and brokenness. Grace, love, forgiveness and patience are the glue of an inclusive community.

Here is my point this whole inclusive thing is going to be uncomfortable for a lot of people because the gospel is blind to the social standards of men and will go after anyone and everyone. The way to cultivate an inclusive community is to embrace the discomfort…. that's right… celebrate it. Tell the church that we are being built like a magnificent temple, not with bricks that are uniformed, square and perfect, but with uniquely misshaped stones that come in all different shapes and sizes, each one being placed into community by the divine builder of the ecclesia, Jesus.

3.   Understand mutual brokenness.

Most people outside the church think that church is the gathering of the good on the Sunday, and if I'm not good then I don't belong there. But the truth is the church is actually the gathering of the guilty, the mutually broken. Why is this so important to remember and recall as followers of Christ? Because if we think we are one hundred percent fixed the chances are we will use our perfection to lord it over others. Even Paul the apostle refers to himself as not having arrived yet (Philippians 3:12) he knows that sanctification is a life long journey. As I mentioned already in this book, salvation is a moment but transformation is a journey. In order to deal with the struggle with inclusion we must constantly remind our community that we are still all mutually broken people. There are still so many parts of our lives that God is still working on by his grace and through his Holy Spirit. For the record what I'm not saying is that we should all consider ourselves as worms and never forget it. NO. To recognize the state of our own brokenness produces compassion and mercy in us. When we really realize how broken we still are and how much compassion and mercy we still need, we can't help but give it to others. If we are all still on the journey of allowing Christ to renew and restore us then we will not just share in understanding one another we will also share compassion and mercy with one another. In his book 'Life Together', Dietrich Bonhoeffer writes it this way:

"IF MY SINFULNESS APPEARS TO ME IN ANY WAY SMALLER OR LESS DETESTABLE IN COMPARISON WITH THE SINS OF OTHERS, I AM STILL NOT RECOGNIZING MY SINFULNESS AT ALL."

The serious state of sin should humble us not cause us to compare sins. The point where you will struggle with inclusion the most is when your sin looks different to other people's sin. We are afraid of what is different. But when we come to the conclusion that sin is sin and Jesus died for ALL sin, we can invite and include everyone to come and bask under the ceaseless flow of God's amazing grace. Our brokenness may look different, but brokenness is brokenness and grace is grace.

4. The journey of patience and the commitment to stay the course.

When we started our church I have to admit I had a very 'Disneyland idea' of how the church would be. I imagined that as soon as we preached the gospel hundreds would flock into the church almost unable to control the urge to surrender their lives to Jesus and allow him to sanctify them through and through. It was going to be a utopia of loving harmonious community, but I found out quickly that it doesn't quite roll out like that. Our vision is to be strictly inclusive, but the reality is it will be a long journey of patience and commitment if we want to get there. If you are truly going to go 'all in' on creating a strictly inclusive community you are going to have to commit to constantly preach, teach and model it. As much as you will preach and teach about being an inclusive community it still won't always sink in. I have had to have difficult conversations with people, even leaders, in our church because while they verbalize their agreement with the message of inclusivity their lives don't match up. You will always find 'clichés' starting to form, because people always lean towards comfort and being an inclusive community isn't always comfortable. We often say in our team meetings that we are 'experts in unfamiliar conversations.' We look out to meet people we have never met before. This type of culture isn't something that forms overnight it takes constant reiteration and sometimes difficult conversations. The difficult conversations are necessary because we can never compromise on the culture of gospel inclusiveness. An inclusive community is a commitment to a life long cultural journey, but the fruit of it will create a culture that reflects Christ and ultimately sees more and more people established in Christ centered community.

CHAPTER THIRTEEN

Who Belongs?

"Therefore, accept each other just as Christ has accepted you so that God will be given glory." (Romans 15:7 NLT)

I love vacations, I'm pretty sure I've never met anyone who doesn't, but I have to say the best type of vacation is the vacation you don't have to pay for. If you're like me you may have been blessed to marry a person whose parents are extremely generous when it comes to paying for family holidays. They have taken us on so many great trips. One glorious day my parents invited us over and sat us down and told us they were going to take us for a three-week trip around Europe, all expense paid! I said let me pray about it... UM YES!

The time came to leave and we arrived at the airport only to find that our seats were no longer available and unfortunately we are going to... wait for it...bump you to FIRST CLASS! I said let me pray about it UM HECK YES! I don't know if you have ever flown first class but let me tell you that if you can't afford to keep flying first class don't do it. Once you have tasted and seen that first class is good, you don't ever want to return to cattle class. I am actually convinced that the inspiration for the design of first class came straight from the book of Leviticus and the tabernacle blue prints. First of all there is a curtain, and when you go through it it's almost like you've entered the holy of holies, I almost wore a rope around my ankle just incase I dropped dead and they had to drag me out! When you get to your seat, it's not actually a seat it's more like a plush leather lounge that happens to turn into a fully reclining bed. I didn't even sleep, because why would you waste your time sleeping! I just lay there enjoying every moment. We finally landed in Rome and we were quick to get amongst all the tourist activities. I am an ancient history fanatic, especially church history (as I previously mentioned) so we began our journey of checking out the sites of the ancient church world of Rome. Our adventures brought us to the Vatican (aka; the Pope's house). The square leading up to St Peters Basilica is overwhelmingly big but when we arrived it was strangely empty. There were barricades and big screens set up around the place, but not many people around. We wandered up to the massive wooden doors of St Peters Basilica. They kind of reminded me of the entrance to *Jurassic Park*, we pushed open the doors and walked in. To our surprise there was around four hundred people seated in the pews as if they where waiting for a service to start then out of nowhere the Pope walked up on the platform, the Pope!! My mother quickly pulled out her video camera and began to film while commentating as if she was filming a wild life documentary all the while making mum jokes, "There's the Pope, isn't he cute, he must be pretty pope-ular, hehehe." Everyone was looking at us with that 'stupid tourist' look. We stayed and listened to the Pope give a sermon for around forty minutes before we realized we couldn't understand Latin. He hadn't quite finished but we thought we might be able to duck out quickly unnoticed before the service finished. We walked back out through the same doors we came in through only to find that the once empty square outside of the church was now full with over ten thousand plus people and they where all seated looking straight at us!! I got so caught up in the moment I just started waving like the Pope. An old Italian man quickly ran over and reefed us away from the staircase platform. He wasn't happy and in broken English started asking why were we in there, and that we shouldn't be in there. I told him we just walked straight in and that if he has a problem he should take it up with their world-class security. He proceeded to badger us and told us that only fourth generation Roman citizens where allowed to go into that church, then the following words spewed out of his mouth, "YOU DON'T BELONG IN THERE." As he said this it was almost as if the words reverberated in my head and for the first time I thought, is that what it feels like? It begs us to ask the question:

Who does belong in the church?

I think automatically all of us in resounding chorus would answer EVERBODY. If that is the case then when did the reputation of the church change? Truth is most people beyond the walls of the church don't feel like they belong there. Unfortunately the reputation that Jesus died on a cross has somehow been tarnished. When most people view the church they conclude that it's the gathering of the good on a Sunday, and if I'm not good, I do not belong in there. But the church is not a gathering of the good on a Sunday, it's the gathering of the guilty. None of us are good and that's why we come not to show off each other's so called 'goodness' but to enjoy the goodness of God!

Jesus flew in the face of the exclusive church and showed by example that all people belong in the church even before they believe. We must use Jesus' example to examine our churches with:

If we aren't attracting the same type Jesus attracted, then maybe we aren't preaching the same message Jesus preached.

How are we supposed to make people feel like they belong in the church?

Simple, the ministry of reconciliation.

In 2 Corinthians 5:11-21 we see Paul through the inspiration of the Holy Spirit declaring the charge we have all been given as followers of Christ, to become ministers of reconciliation! He goes on to say that because of this ministry we no longer count men's sins against them. Why emphasize not counting sins? Paul understood that what you can count you can measure and what you can measure you can judge. Counting sins will eventually cause us to measure ourselves against other people. Our badness versus their badness! But Scripture levels the playing field and tells us that all have sinned and have fallen short, in other words there is not bad and really bad, we are all bad. In his book *The Prodigal God* Timothy Keller puts it like this:

"THE GOSPEL IS DISTINCT FROM ANY OTHER
RELIGION. IN ITS VIEW, EVERYONE IS WRONG,
EVERYONE IS LOVED, AND EVERYONE IS CALLED
TO RECOGNIZE THIS AND CHANGE."

Because of this we approach people not with a self-righteous approach but a sympathetic approach. We have a lot in common with sinners because we are sinners and the only difference is now we are saved by grace so that no-one can boast that they save themselves.

So why should I accept other people?

In order to effectively love and include the people around us, even the ones we don't particularly like, we must first come to Christ's acceptance of us. Take a moment to run through the archives of your life and see all the bad and the ugly things you have ever done to others, or thought, or didn't do. We would all conclude that none of us would like for those things to be live fed onto a huge cinema screen for all our friends, family or general public to watch. Yet Christ sees them all, everything is laid bare before him, even the things we are yet to do, he sees it (Hebrews 4:13), and despite all that, Christ accepts us.

So now we accept each other the way Christ accepted us. Without judgment or conditions, with our prejudice or preconceived ideas. Christ is the filter that we pour everyone through. We accept others the way Christ accepted us.

When Jesus comes back for his church, it will be filled with the socially rejected, the outcast, the hurt and the broken, the ones who know they haven't got it together, but have dared to trust in the radical grace of God.

One of my favorite books is the '*Ragga-muffin Gospel*' by Brennan Manning, he brilliantly describes the mission and the membership of the church:

"JESUS COMES NOT FOR THE SUPER-SPIRITUAL, BUT

FOR THE WOBBLY AND THE WEAK-KNEED WHO KNOW
THEY DON'T HAVE IT ALL TOGETHER, AND WHO
ARE NOT TOO PROUD TO ACCEPT THE HANDOUT
OF AMAZING GRACE... SOMETHING IS RADICALLY
WRONG WHEN THE LOCAL CHURCH REJECTS A
PERSON WHO IS ACCEPTED BY JESUS... ANY CHURCH
THAT WILL NOT ACCEPT THAT IT CONSISTS OF
SINFUL MEN AND WOMEN, AND EXISTS FOR THEM,
IMPLICITLY REJECTS THE GOSPEL OF GRACE."[1]

In echoing this beautiful quote I want to describe what I believe a
'Strictly Inclusive' church should look like.

1. It is real.

In a world bombarded with a love for social media, Instagram,
Facebook, and so forth, we have become experts in the art of
projecting what we want people to see and not actually showing
who we really are. The danger is we have gone so far down the
rabbit hole of phony persona that we don't know how to be real
anymore. On top of that we have become afraid that if we reveal
who we really are others won't accept us. So we just keep up
with the façade. It's so much more freeing to be real before God
because fakeness is like a stage act that never ends. How freeing
it is to know that Jesus didn't come for who we pretend to be,
Jesus came for who we really are. The people who encountered
grace the quickest were the ones who where most open about
the realness of there issues, the prostitute, the tax collector, the
greedy little rich man, the demoniac man. They all knew how
real their problems were and they knew how real amazing grace
was, how much they needed it, and how freely it flowed from
Jesus. A strictly inclusive church must promote realness for when
we are truly real and honest about our sin, failings, insecurities,
fears, it's in that place that God's grace becomes amazing. A real

Who Belongs?

church is full of real people with real problems who journey with other people with real problems, towards the God of real grace, real forgiveness and real fulfillment.

2. It's raw.

We have all prayed prayers like, 'Lord fill your church' or 'Lord help us to reach those far from you', but my question is, are we really ready for what we are praying for? What I've found to be true is that when people arrive in our churches they don't come prefabricated and perfect. If anything, they come in as raw material. To be a strictly inclusive church we must ask ourselves are we ready for raw? We should be - that's what discipleship and being a disciple of Jesus is all about. I love the story of Lazarus and his resurrection in John 11. Jesus arrives at the tomb and what we see is an actual resurrection taking place. But what we also must take note of some sorts, is what Jesus' role is on the earth today, and also what our role is as disciples working alongside Jesus. Jesus says to the dead man, "Lazarus come forth" and he does, he comes back to life. In the same way salvation is the spiritual reality of people who are dead in their sins coming to life in Christ. But what is interesting to note is that Jesus doesn't stop there, he turns to his disciples and says, "Roll away the stone" and "Take off his grave clothes." Jesus is the resurrection, He is the savior, but we are the stone-rollers and the removers of grave clothes. So often the church has been known for throwing stones of judgment and of condemnation. Whereas God has called us to roll away stones. The stones of miss-perception, the stones of inconvenience, the stones that stop people from getting to Jesus! Once the stones have been removed and we find these precious lives coming into our churches and social circles it is our job to help in the removal of grave clothes. I have seen first hand when people come to church in their raw state, Christians have been quick to judge them by there grave clothes. We see the length of a girl's skirt or lack thereof and become quick to judge what type of person she must be. We overlook that although she is in church in a skimpy outfit she was only six months ago wearing nothing allowing herself to be used by men in order to try and find affirmation from a man. But PRAISE GOD, she may be in church scantily dressed but at least she is one step closer to finding affirmation from her heavenly Father. We see the disheveled man smoking out front of the church and we hear the murmur of the so-called religious elite question why this man is smoking the 'devil's sticks' out in front of the church. But PRAISE GOD he is smoking out in front of the church because a few months ago he was smoking crack cocaine under a bridge in order to escape the memory of his horrific past. But now he is one step closer to One who redeems the past and gives us a glorious future. We must always remember that beneath the grave clothes is a precious life Jesus died for. Yes it can be hard to handle raw people but then again we were raw once, and someone by the grace of God journeyed with us, helping us to remove our grave clothes. If we were all truly honest with ourselves we would all have to admit that there are still some items of grave clothing we are still working on removing. The truth be told, raw churches are all that there are. We just need to recognize that rawness comes in different packages, none worse than the other, just different.

3. It's relentlessly inclusive.

I think most churches want and plan to be inclusive. When you study and preach the gospel you can't help but be compelled by the example of Jesus to include the excluded, but how long does it last? Does our inclusivity have a shelf life? At what point do we throw in the towel? To be an inclusive church is not a once-off occasion or a seasonal focus it's a cultural foundation in which we build everything on. To be relentless in our inclusivity is to, with all passion and intentionality, beat the drum of the inclusive grace of God and let that sound echo through every aspect of our church.

A strictly inclusive church is full of beautiful and rich diversity:

We have ex-drug addicts sitting next to ex-people pleasing addicts. We have ex-convicted criminals sitting next to ex-convicted hypocrites.

We have those who are physically crippled on the outside sitting next to those who are emotionally crippled on the inside.

But here we are just a bunch of misfits who have arrived on the doorstep of grace who found ourselves included in the love of Christ, and invited to journey with him into the future. Where: healing is inevitable. Wholeness is a promise, joy is a gift, fulfillment is received and His grace is sufficient .

I have a friend named Pete. Pete is a member of our church but he wasn't always. Pete had spent most of his teenage life on the streets. He fell into a pretty serious drug addiction and through a series of events was in and out of jail. The last time he came out of jail he decided to move to Cronulla in Sydney. One Sunday afternoon he was walking by a local park and noticed a building. A huge banner was strung up to the outside wall, with huge bold black letters that read "WELCOME." It was our church. He walked inside and was overwhelmed by the love and acceptance of what was then just a group of strangers. During a Wednesday night prayer meeting Pete came up to me and told me something I will never forget. "James, I've drunken a six pack of wild turkey and gone through a whole packet of cigarettes, but I still knew I could come to church." My heart leapt in that moment. Why? Because the true inclusive message of the gospel had gotten through! Pete knew that regardless of his struggles, he could still come to church. He could still approach the throne of grace with confidence. Pete's journey since coming to our church. has been full of ups and downs, but he will tell you that he is not the person he was before. The transforming power of God is changing him into the person God destined him to be. The point is no-one comes pre-fabricated and perfect. Our inclusivity cannot be restricted to a short span of time. We must be committed to journeying with people through the thick and the thin, the highs and the lows. Inclusion must be like God's love... relentless.

The nature of the gospel is and will always be inclusive. If the gospel is inclusive the church must reflect that nature, not just the theory but in practice. I will finish this book with a closing statement that basically sums up this whole book:

'The gospel is one big open invitation to a party intended for all. The dress code is the real you. You don't have to bring a gift, as it will be provided for you when you arrive. You come in through gates of God's goodness, and then walk through the beautifully welcoming doors of repentance. The theme of the party is love and mercy, and the host of the celebration is Jesus. The gift you receive is God's grace and forgiveness, and you are welcomed to sit at a never ending table of fellowship with God your creator. There are reserved seats all around you, which have been left for your friends, your family, your enemies and complete strangers, who you have been encouraged to invite and share the party with. You have been invited to invite, included to include, and loved to show love. It is Strictly Inclusive.'

God bless you.

James Murray

James Murray and his wife Alanna and their three beautiful kids live in Sydney and are the lead pastors of C3 Church Cronulla, situated in the heart of the Sutherland Shire. James has been a sought-after communicator of the Gospel in church circles all around the world for many years. His passion is preaching the inclusive love of Jesus to anyone and everyone.